YOUNG LEARNER'S ATLAS

Written by:
Kay Barnham
and
Robin Lawrie

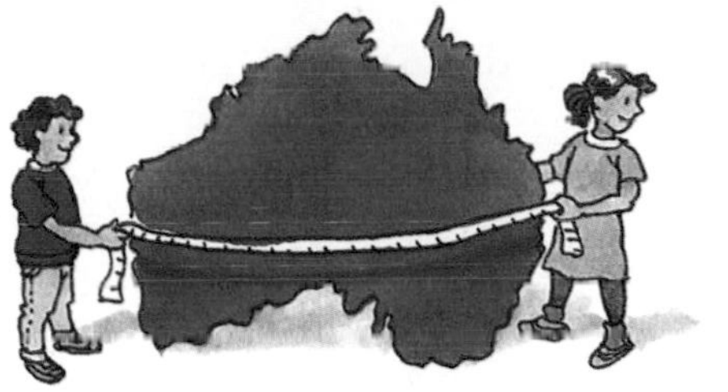

Illustrated by:
Robin
Lawrie

www.alligatorbooks.co.uk

Published by
Alligator Books Limited
Gadd House
Arcadia Avenue
London N3 2JU

Written by Kay Barnham & Robin Lawrie
Illustrated by Robin Lawrie
Printed in China

YOUNG LEARNER'S ATLAS

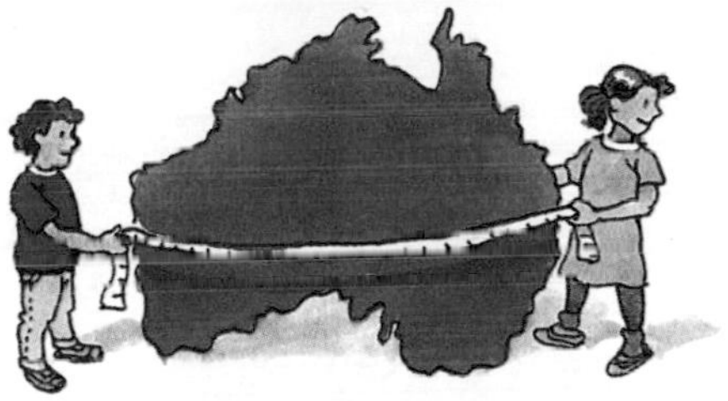

Contents

All About Maps

A map is a picture of a place seen from far above.

A book of maps is called an atlas. It shows maps of every country in the world.

Watch for the mini-map of the world to see where each country belongs.

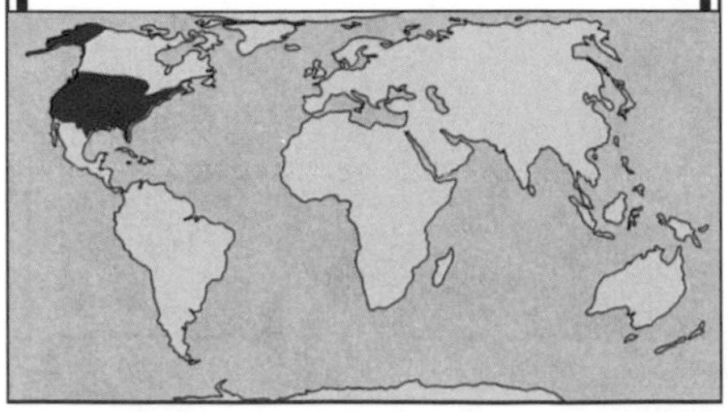

Maps can show places from near or far away.

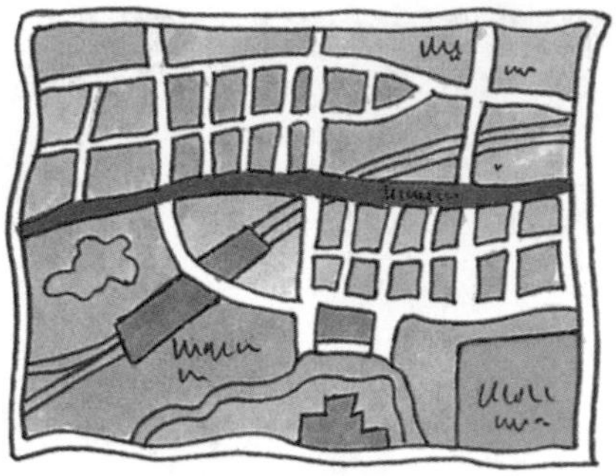

Some maps are so detailed that they show all the streets in a town or city.

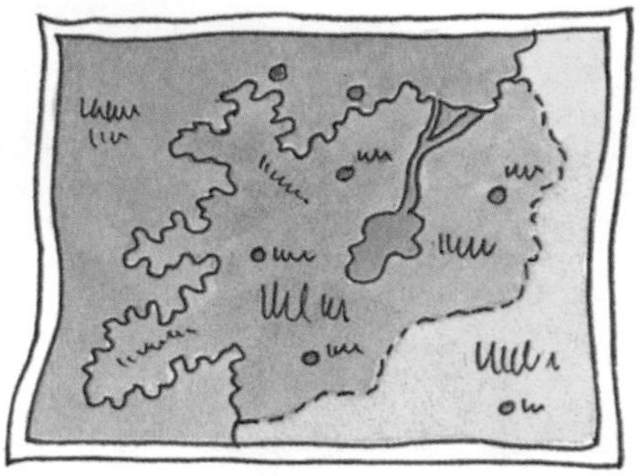

Maps of whole countries are shown from far away. Dots show where towns and cities are.

Maps cannot copy the real size of the places they show. They are drawn to a scale, which means that they are shrunk to fit the page.

Miles	250	500	1000
Kilometres	250	500	1000

A small distance on a map stands for a much larger distance in real life. The distance is shown under each map on a scale bar, which shows miles and kilometres.

The symbols below are used on the maps in this book.

Borders 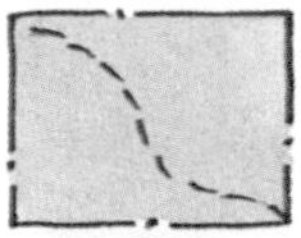

Capital cities 

Large cities 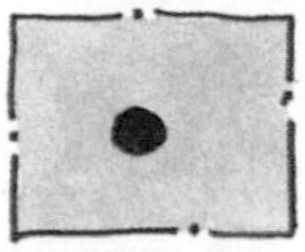

Lakes 

Rivers 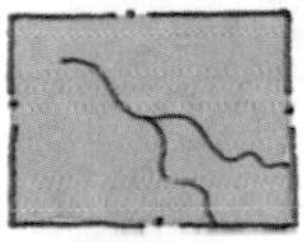

Oceans and seas 

Mountains 

Find out where different animals live in the world. Look for them on each map.

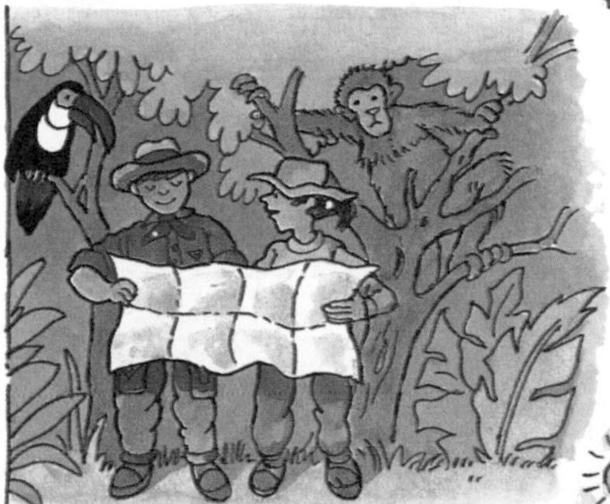

Explorers and travellers use maps to find their way.

You can use maps to see where you live in the world, or perhaps where you are going on holiday.

The index on page 40 has an alphabetical list of all the countries in the world. It tells you where to find each country in this atlas.

There is a compass beside every map in this book. This is to show you in which direction the map is facing.

North points to the top of the world and South points to the bottom of the world.

WORLD MAP

This is what the world would look like if it were flattened out. The seven coloured areas are called continents.

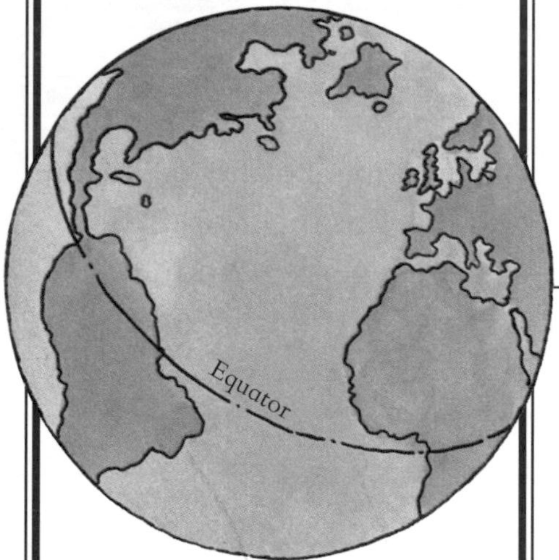

Equator

The Equator is an imaginary line running round the middle of the world, which divides it into northern and southern hemispheres. Europe is in the northern hemisphere.

North America stretches from the Arctic almost to the Equator.

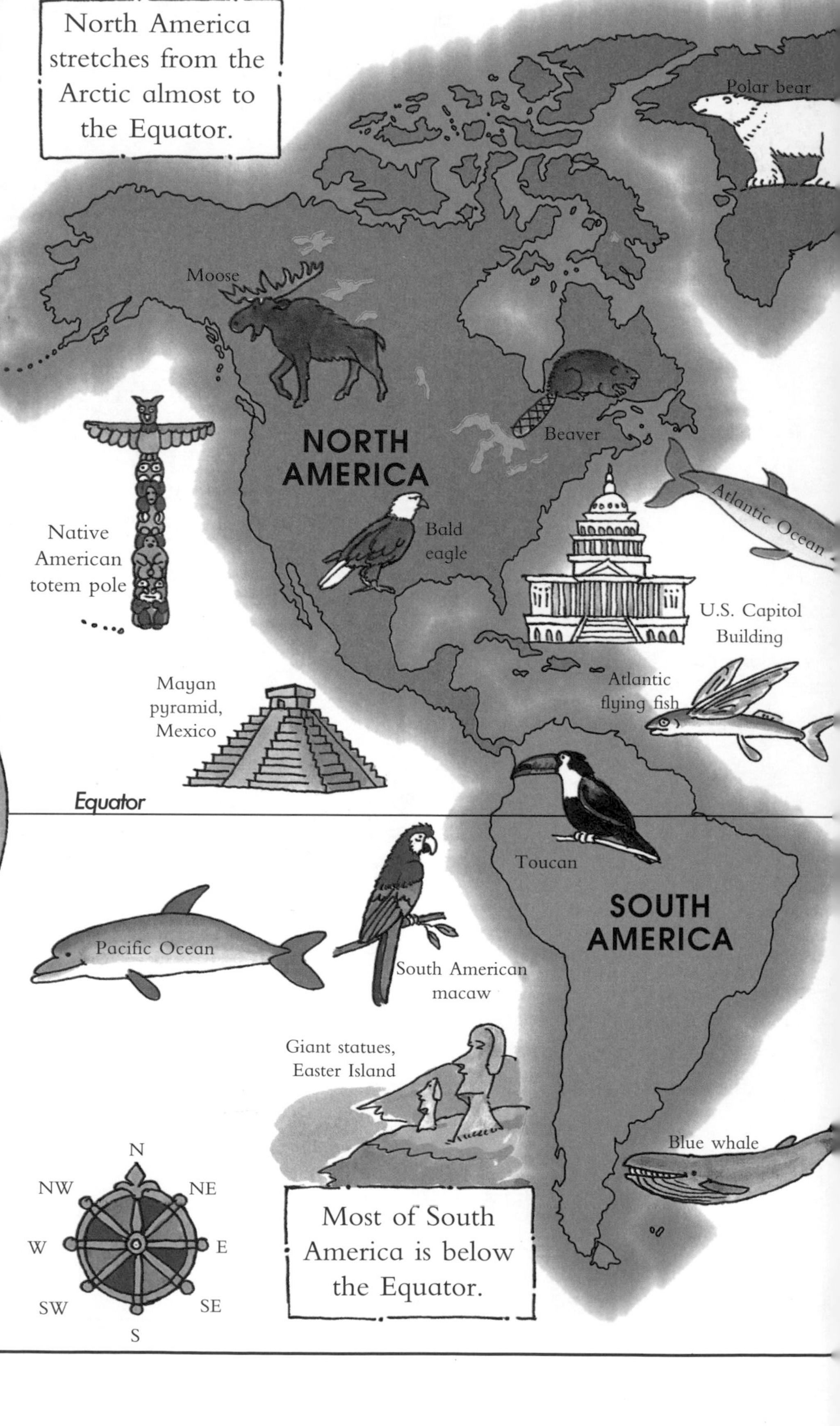

Polar bear
Moose
Beaver
NORTH AMERICA
Atlantic Ocean
Native American totem pole
Bald eagle
U.S. Capitol Building
Mayan pyramid, Mexico
Atlantic flying fish
Equator
Toucan
SOUTH AMERICA
Pacific Ocean
South American macaw
Giant statues, Easter Island
Blue whale
N
NE
E
SE
S
SW
W
NW

Most of South America is below the Equator.

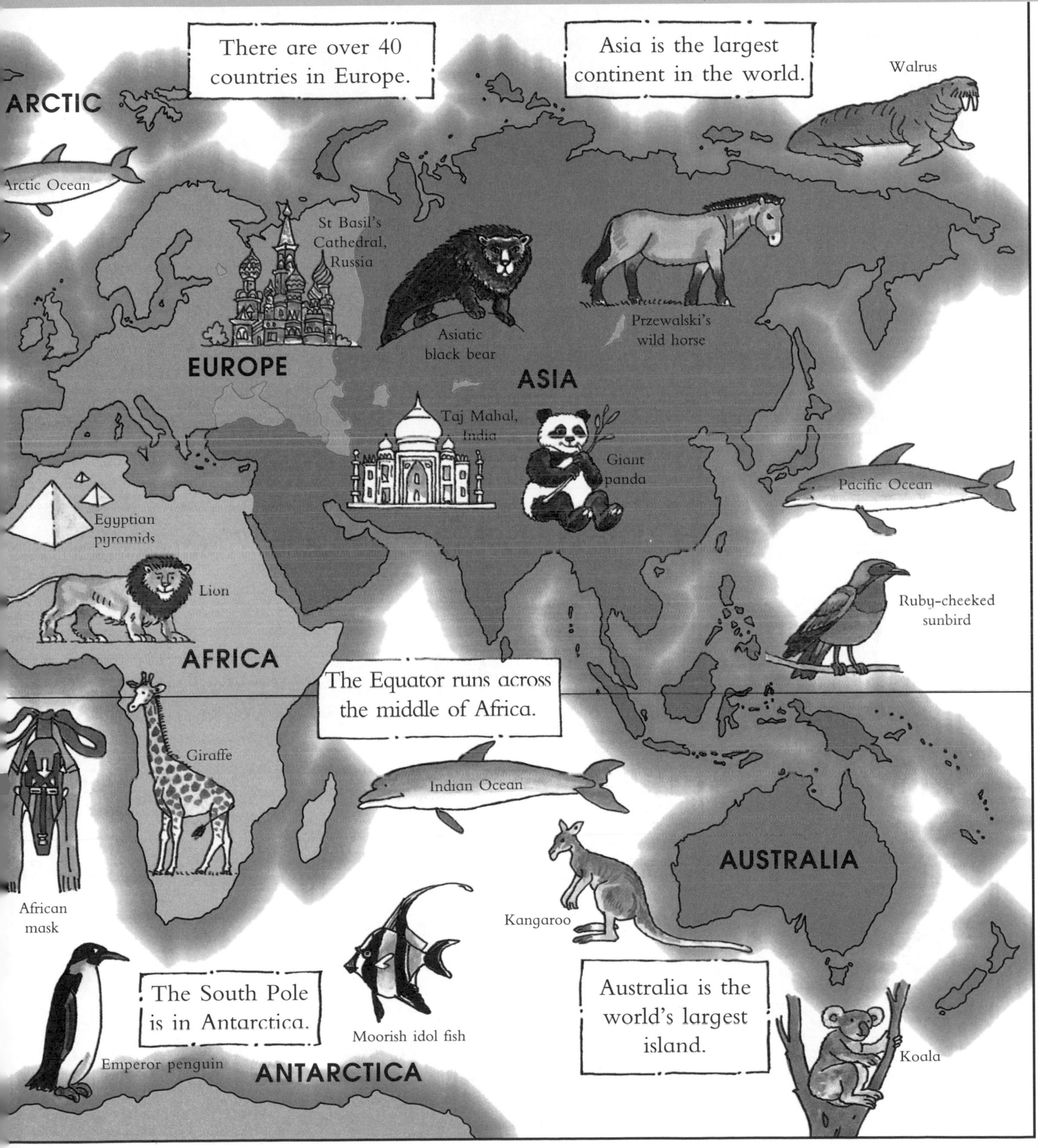
There are over 40 countries in Europe.
Asia is the largest continent in the world.
Walrus
ARCTIC
Arctic Ocean
St Basil's Cathedral, Russia
Asiatic black bear
Przewalski's wild horse
EUROPE
ASIA
Taj Mahal, India
Giant panda
Pacific Ocean
Egyptian pyramids
Lion
Ruby-cheeked sunbird
AFRICA
The Equator runs across the middle of Africa.
Giraffe
Indian Ocean
AUSTRALIA
African mask
Kangaroo
The South Pole is in Antarctica.
Moorish idol fish
Australia is the world's largest island.
Koala
Emperor penguin
ANTARCTICA

AROUND THE WORLD

The surface of the Earth is different all over the world. More than two-thirds is covered with water. Inside the Earth there are layers. As these move, heat can build up and cause volcanic eruptions.

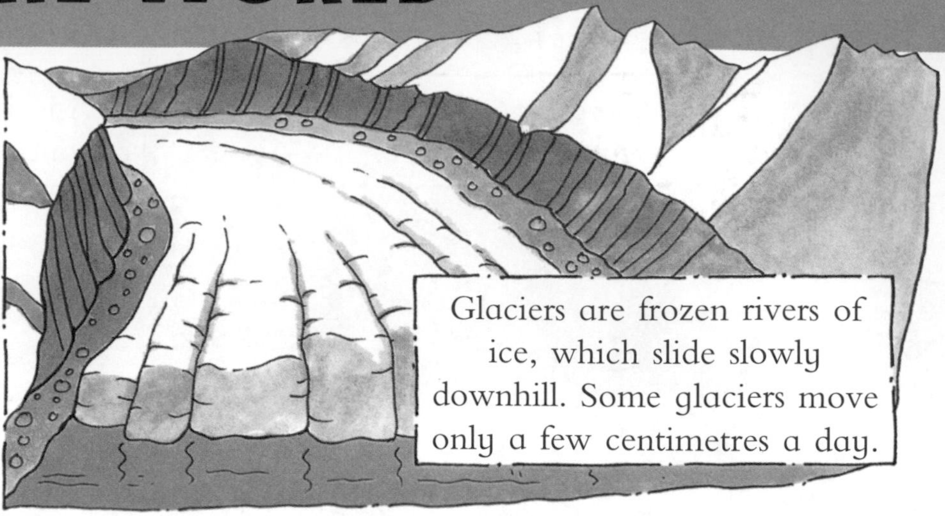

Glaciers are frozen rivers of ice, which slide slowly downhill. Some glaciers move only a few centimetres a day.

Canyons are formed when rivers slowly wash away the rock. The Grand Canyon, in the USA, is more than a mile deep!

Geysers are hot springs that shoot hot water into the air. The most famous geyser, 'Old Faithful', is in Yellowstone Park, USA.

Coral reefs are formed in warm, shallow seas from the skeletons of millions of tiny sea creatures. The Great Barrier Reef, in Australia, is the largest.

Deserts are very dry places where only a little rain falls. Only a few plants and animals can survive. Camels can live for many days without water.

A waterfall is where a river crashes down a steep slope. Angel Falls in Venezuela is higher than the tallest building in the world.

Rivers can form when rainwater flows down a slope. The ground wears away and the river gets deeper and wider.

Mountains are rocky peaks that rise high above the ground. Some of the highest are found under the sea.

When a volcano erupts, hot liquid rock, called lava, shoots into the air in the form of fine ash. After eruption, a volcano may stay active or never erupt again.

Earthquakes shake the ground. When an earthquake occurs under the sea, it makes a huge ocean wave called a tsunami.

Rainforests grow near the Equator. Rain falls there nearly every day. Lots of animals live in the tall treetops.

In North America, grassland is called prairie, while in South America it is called pampas. It is used for grazing animals and growing crops.

The Changing World

The Earth was formed more than 4.5 billion years ago. Its surface was molten rock.

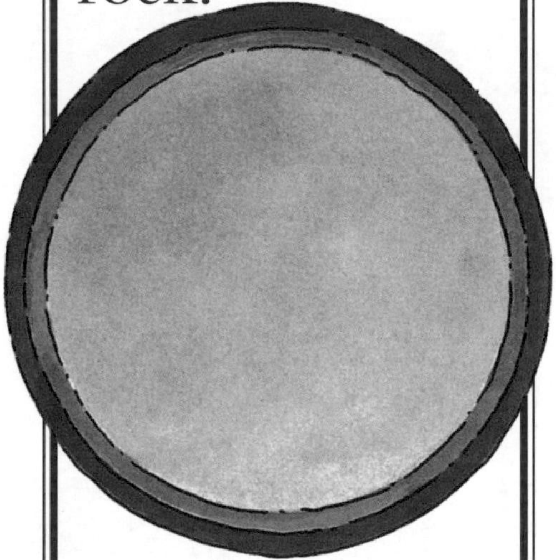

Rain cooled and hardened the Earth. The water formed shallow seas.

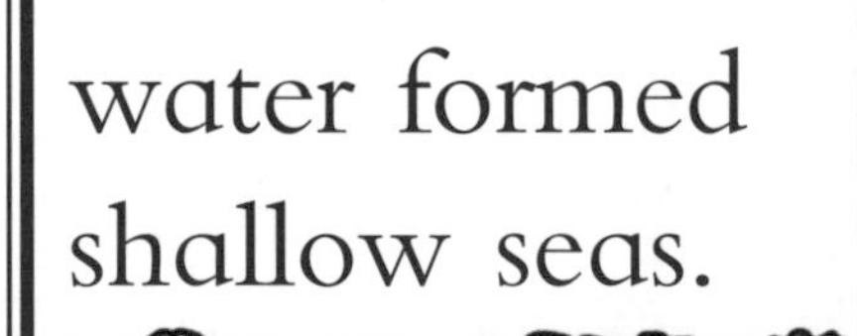

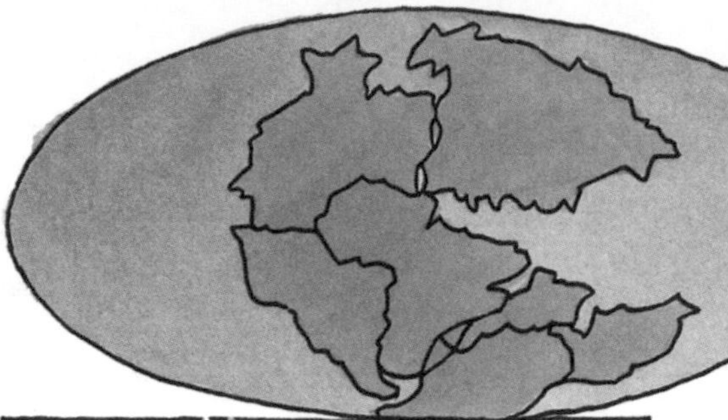

About 200 million years ago the continents were all joined together and surrounded by one vast ocean.

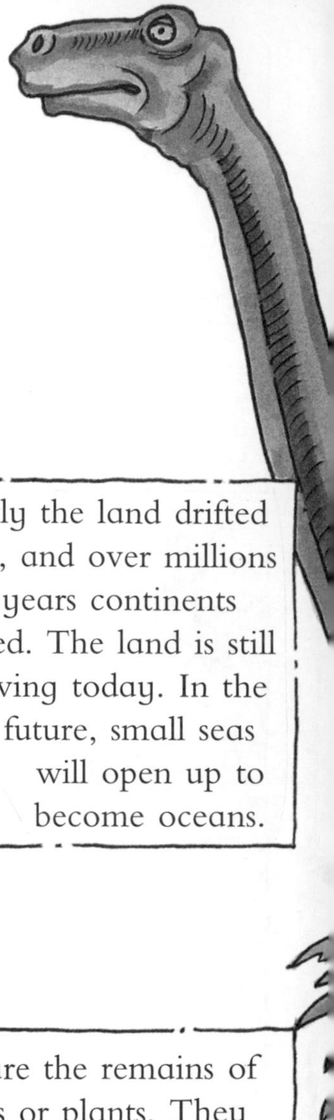

Slowly the land drifted apart, and over millions of years continents formed. The land is still moving today. In the future, small seas will open up to become oceans.

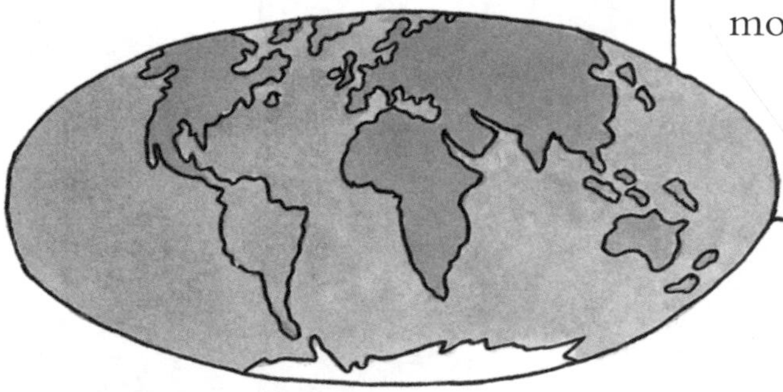

Large chunks of land, called plates, move by floating on a layer of hot, molten rock.

Fossils are the remains of animals or plants. They help us find out about living things from long ago.

The first animals lived in the sea. Then, animals that could live both in the sea and on land developed. Eventually, some animals began to live only on land.

Dinosaurs died out 65 million years ago. Early humans did not appear until four million years ago.

Dinosaurs were early animals. The biggest dinosaurs were plant-eaters and needed long necks to reach leaves in the treetops. Diplodocus's neck was 10 metres long.

Over many years animals gradually change. This is called evolution. This helps them to survive better in their surroundings.

People of the World

Here you can see traditional costumes that are still worn on special festival days around the world. Learn how people say "hello" in different languages, too.

There are over 5,000 languages. If you learn to speak different languages, you can speak to people all around the world.

France
"Bonjour" (French)
Italy
"Ciao" (Italian)
Denmark
"Halloj" (Danish)
Poland
"Dzien dobry" (Polish)
Greece
"Yia sas" (Greek)
India
"Namaste" (Hindi)

Some alphabets use different letters, and Chinese and Japanese alphabets have 'picture writing' instead. There are over 65 different alphabets.

ΣΩΘ ЖИФ

Some languages are spoken in many places. Spanish is widely spoken in South American countries because many settlers came from Spain.

Traditional clothes are still worn in some countries. Inuit people in the Arctic wear fur to keep warm. Loose cotton clothes keep Africans and Indians cool in the hot sun.

EUROPE

Europe is about the same size as the USA, but has nearly three times as many people. There are many different cultures and more than 40 languages are spoken.

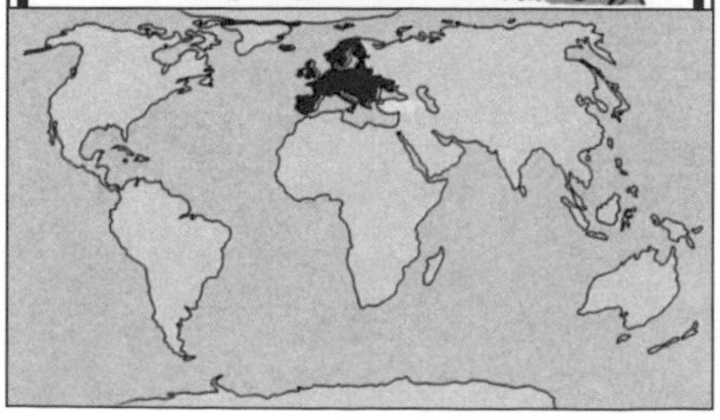

The Netherlands is known for growing beautiful tulips.

Swiss clockmakers are famous for their skills.

Historic Britain has many famous landmarks.

Highland dancing

Many famous painters lived in France. The country is well known for its wine and cheese.

Flamenco dancers

Leaning Tower of Pisa, Italy

MILES	250	500	1000	
KILOMETRES	500	1000	1500	2000

Highest mountain: Mount Elbrus, Russia, 5,633 m.

Longest river: River Volga, Russia, 3,531 km.

Weather: Northern Europe is cool but the south is warm in summer.

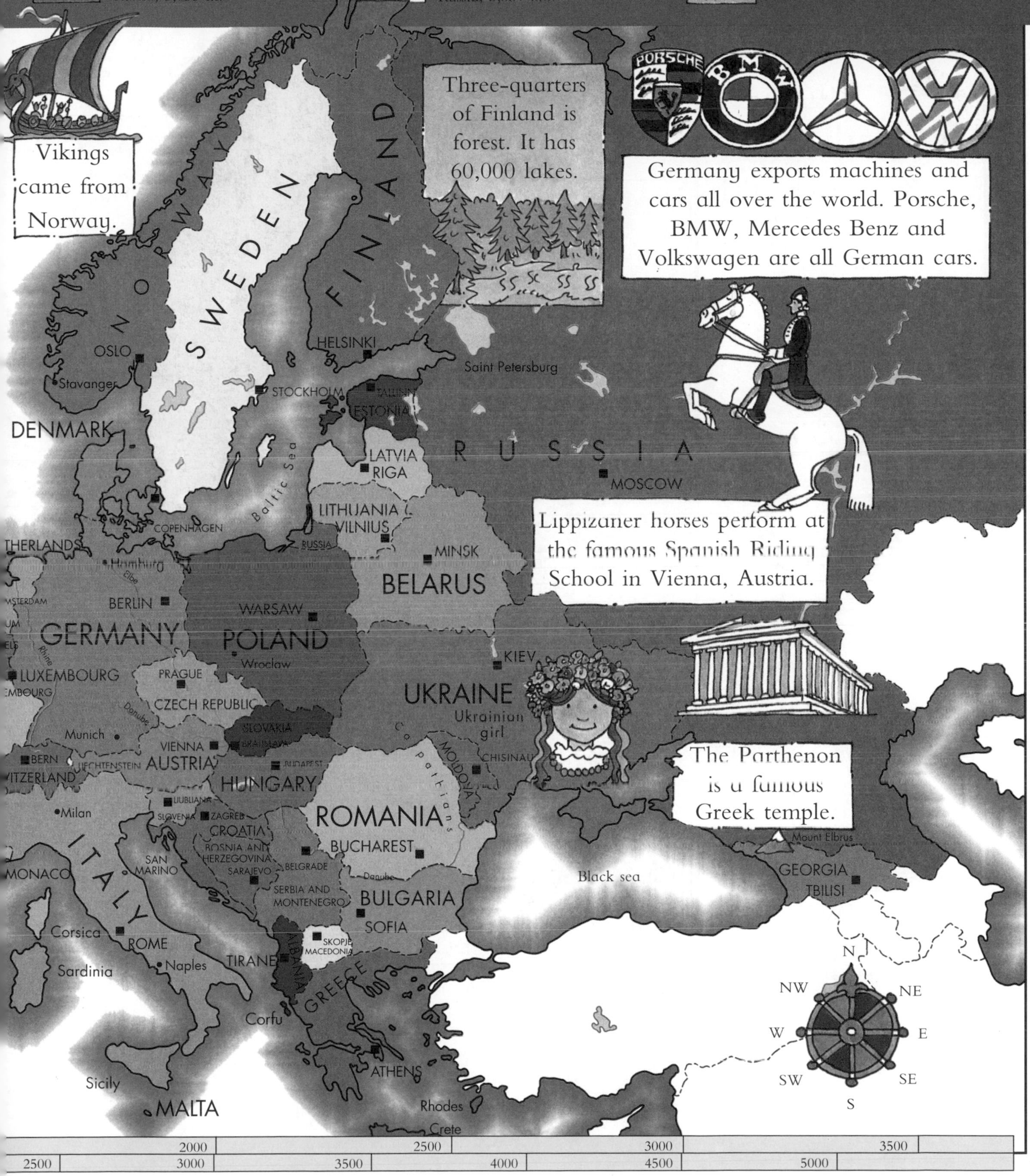

Vikings came from Norway.
Three-quarters of Finland is forest. It has 60,000 lakes.
PORSCHE
BMW
Germany exports machines and cars all over the world. Porsche, BMW, Mercedes Benz and Volkswagen are all German cars.
Lippizaner horses perform at the famous Spanish Riding School in Vienna, Austria.
The Parthenon is a famous Greek temple.
NORWAY
SWEDEN
FINLAND
HELSINKI
OSLO
Stavanger
STOCKHOLM
TALLINN
ESTONIA
Saint Petersburg
DENMARK
RUSSIA
LATVIA
RIGA
MOSCOW
Baltic Sea
COPENHAGEN
LITHUANIA
VILNIUS
RUSSIA
MINSK
BELARUS
Hamburg
Elbe
BERLIN
WARSAW
GERMANY
POLAND
Wroclaw
Rhine
LUXEMBOURG
PRAGUE
CZECH REPUBLIC
KIEV
UKRAINE
Ukrainian girl
Danube
SLOVAKIA
BRATISLAVA
Munich
VIENNA
AUSTRIA
BERN
LIECHTENSTEIN
BUDAPEST
HUNGARY
Carpathians
MOLDOVA
CHISINAU
LJUBLJANA
SLOVENIA
ZAGREB
Milan
CROATIA
ROMANIA
BOSNIA AND HERZEGOVINA
SARAJEVO
BELGRADE
BUCHAREST
SAN MARINO
MONACO
ITALY
SERBIA AND MONTENEGRO
Danube
BULGARIA
SOFIA
Black sea
GEORGIA
TBILISI
Mount Elbrus
Corsica
ROME
SKOPJE
MACEDONIA
Sardinia
Naples
TIRANE
ALBANIA
GREECE
Corfu
ATHENS
Sicily
MALTA
Rhodes
Crete
N
NW
NE
W
E
SW
SE
S
2000
2500
3000
3500
2500
3000
3500
4000
4500
5000

CIS

CIS stands for the Commonwealth of Independent States. It was formed from parts of the Union of Soviet Socialist Republics in 1991.

Russia is the biggest country in the world.

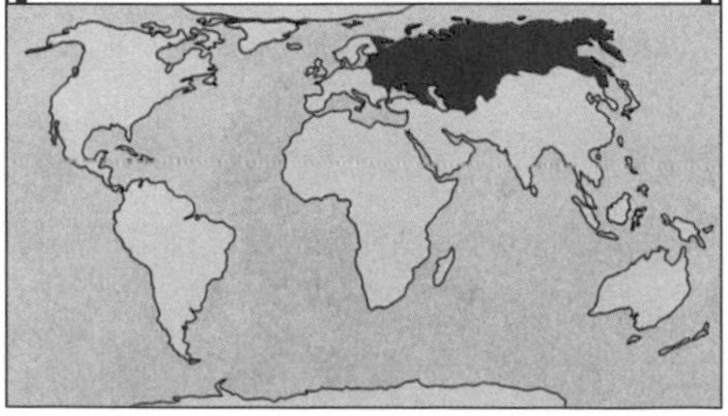

Moscow is the home of the famous Bolshoi Ballet dancers. They have performed all over the world.

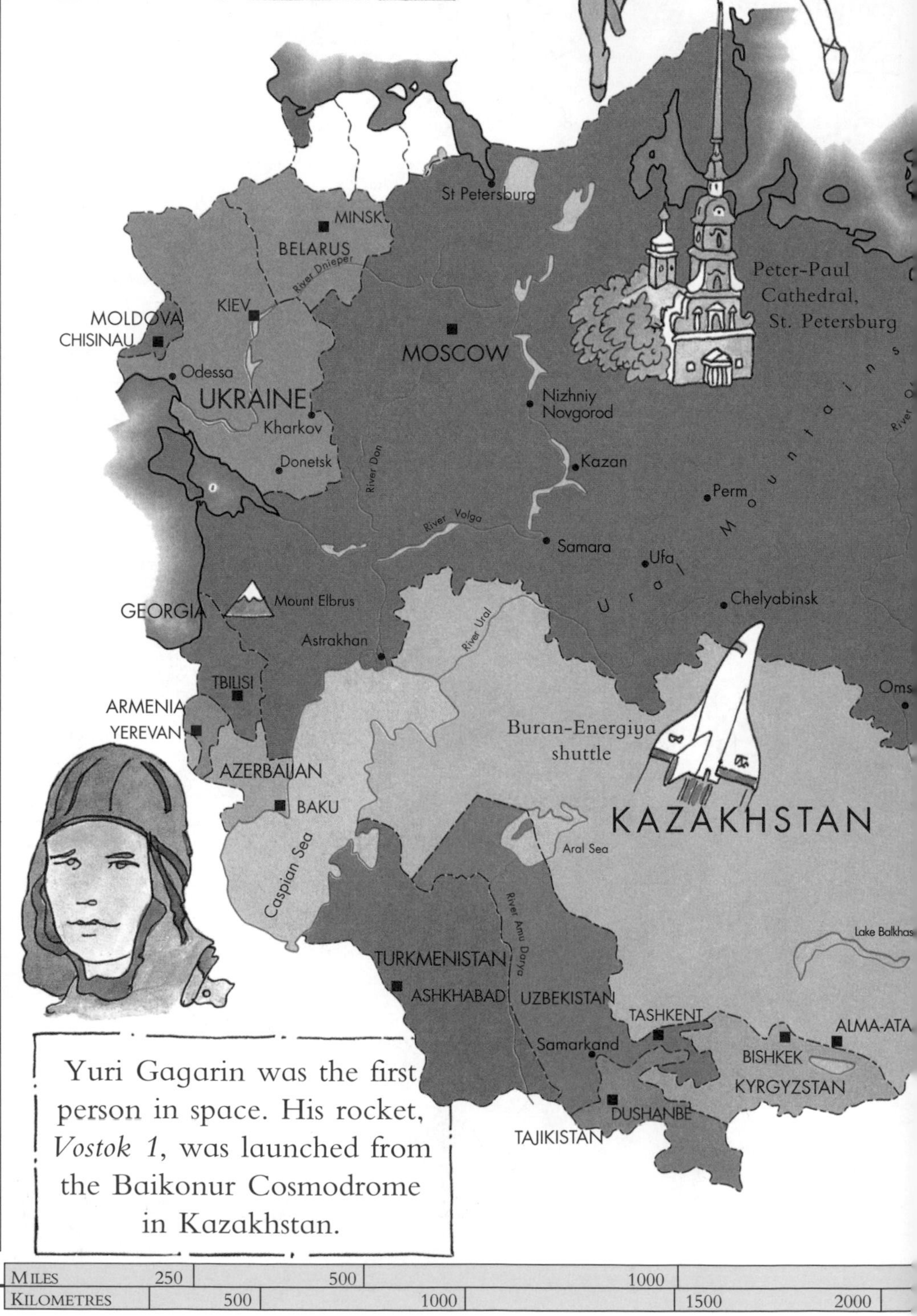

St Petersburg
MINSK
BELARUS
River Dnieper
KIEV
MOLDOVA
CHISINAU
Odessa
UKRAINE
Kharkov
Donetsk
MOSCOW
Nizhniy Novgorod
Kazan
River Don
River Volga
Samara
Perm
Ufa
Ural Mountains
Chelyabinsk
Peter-Paul Cathedral, St. Petersburg
River Ob
Mount Elbrus
GEORGIA
Astrakhan
River Ural
TBILISI
ARMENIA
YEREVAN
AZERBAIJAN
BAKU
Buran-Energiya shuttle
KAZAKHSTAN
Oms
Aral Sea
Caspian Sea
River Amu Darya
Lake Balkhash
TURKMENISTAN
ASHKHABAD
UZBEKISTAN
TASHKENT
ALMA-ATA
Samarkand
BISHKEK
KYRGYZSTAN
DUSHANBE
TAJIKISTAN
Miles 250 500 1000
Kilometres 500 1000 1500 2000

Yuri Gagarin was the first person in space. His rocket, *Vostok 1*, was launched from the Baikonur Cosmodrome in Kazakhstan.

Arctic Ocean

The north is very cold in the winter months. Temperatures in Siberia can sometimes reach -60°C.

The Siberian coast is only 89 kilometres from mainland Alaska.

Severnaya Zemlya

New Siberian Isles

ovaya emlya

Tiger

Cherskiy Mountains

Kolyma Mountains

Kamchatka Peninsula

Icebreaker

Asiatic black bear

Verkhoyansk Mountains

River Lena

R U S S I A

There are over 250 volcanoes on the Kamchatka Peninsula and nearby islands.

River Yenisey

Sable

Russian troika

Sakhalin

Russian sturgeon

Novosibirsk   Krasnoyarsk

Lake Baykal

River Amur

Altai Mountains

Pacific Ocean

Vladivostok

The Trans-Siberian Railway runs from Moscow to Vladivostok. It is the longest railway in the world!

N

NW   NE

W   E

SW   SE

S

Lake Baykal is the deepest lake in the world. One part is 1,940 metres deep!

		2000			2500			3000			3500	
2500		3000		3500		4000		4500		5000		

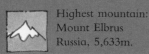

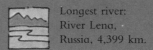

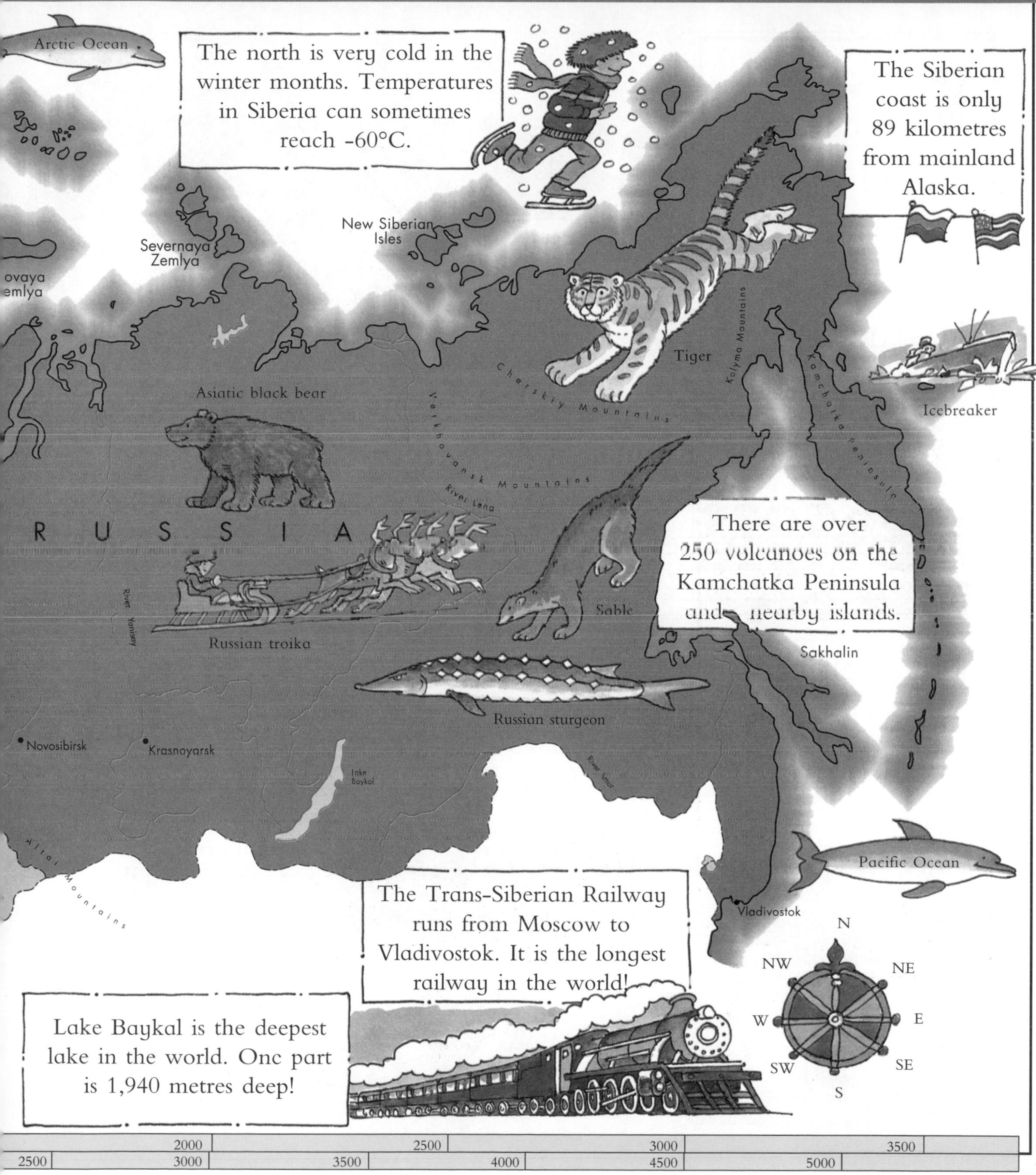

AFRICA

There are about 670 million people in Africa – over twice the number of people in the USA.

The world's largest desert is the Sahara Desert in Africa.

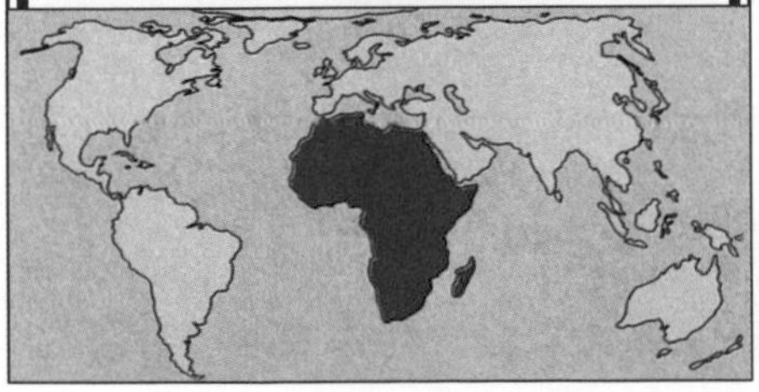

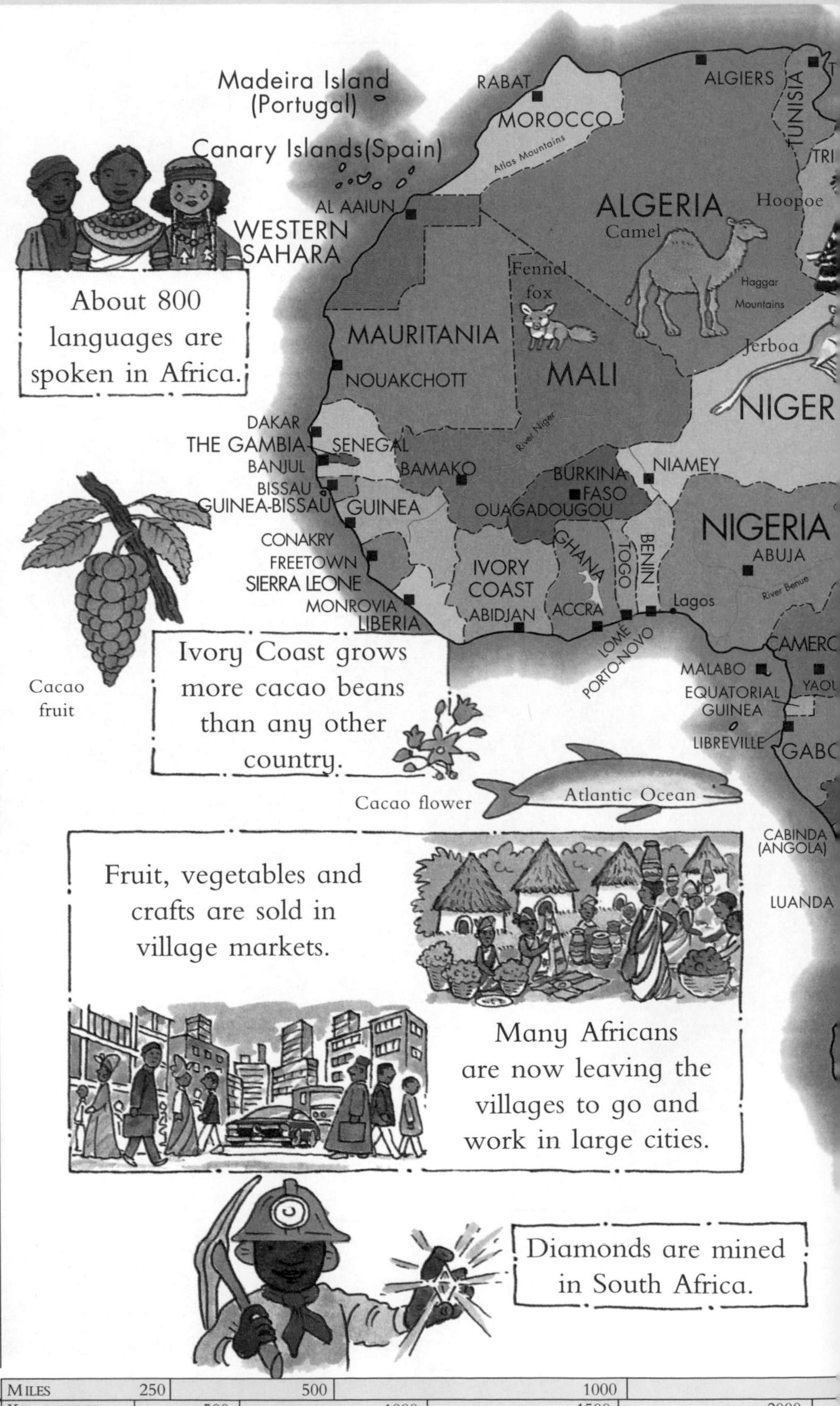

Madeira Island (Portugal)
Canary Islands(Spain)
RABAT
MOROCCO
Atlas Mountains
ALGIERS
TUNISIA
ALGERIA
Camel
Hoopoe
Haggar Mountains
AL AAIUN
WESTERN SAHARA
Fennel fox
MAURITANIA
NOUAKCHOTT
MALI
Jerboa
NIGER
DAKAR
THE GAMBIA
SENEGAL
BANJUL
BAMAKO
River Niger
BISSAU
GUINEA-BISSAU
GUINEA
BURKINA FASO
OUAGADOUGOU
NIAMEY
NIGERIA
ABUJA
River Benue
CONAKRY
FREETOWN
SIERRA LEONE
MONROVIA
LIBERIA
IVORY COAST
ABIDJAN
GHANA
ACCRA
TOGO
LOMÉ
BENIN
PORTO-NOVO
Lagos
MALABO
EQUATORIAL GUINEA
LIBREVILLE
Cacao fruit
Cacao flower
Atlantic Ocean
CABINDA (ANGOLA)
LUANDA
MILES 250 500 1000
KILOMETRES 500 1000 1500 2000

About 800 languages are spoken in Africa.

Ivory Coast grows more cacao beans than any other country.

Fruit, vegetables and crafts are sold in village markets.

Many Africans are now leaving the villages to go and work in large cities.

Diamonds are mined in South Africa.

Highest mountain: Mount Kilimanjaro, Tanzania, 5,895 m.

Longest river: River Nile, Egypt, 6,650 km.

Weather: It is hot and humid at the Equator. The deserts in the north are very hot and dry.

The land around the River Nile is green and fertile. This is the only part of Egypt that can be farmed. The rest is sandy desert.

Africa still has herds of wild animals. They graze on the grasslands of the savannah.

Many wild animals live in wildlife reserves which protect them.

Madagascar is called the 'Red Island' because of its red soil. It is the home of the lemur.

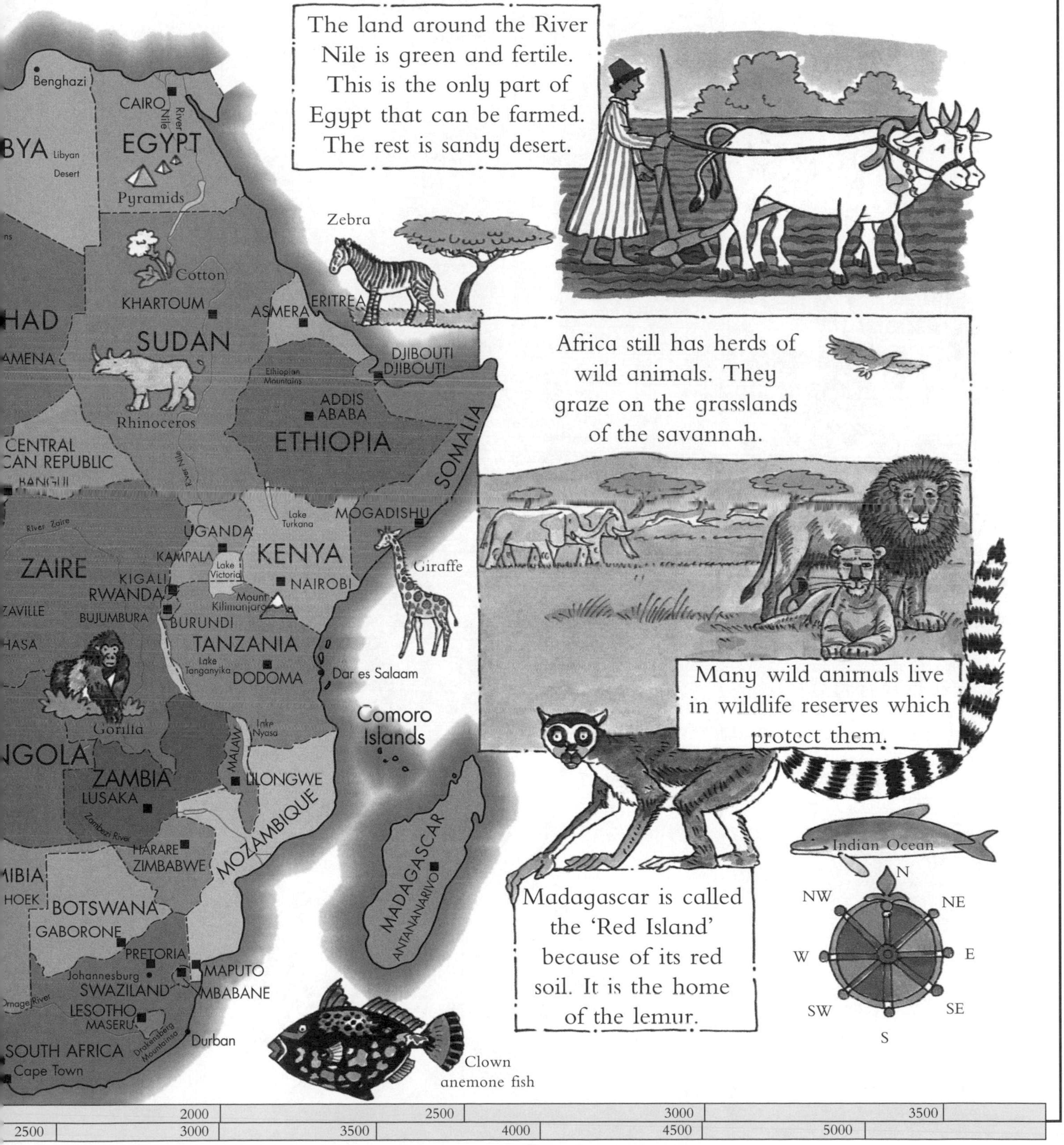

Benghazi
CAIRO
River Nile
BYA
Libyan Desert
EGYPT
Pyramids
Zebra
Cotton
KHARTOUM
ASMERA
ERITREA
HAD
SUDAN
AMENA
DJIBOUTI
DJIBOUTI
Ethiopian Mountains
Rhinoceros
ADDIS ABABA
ETHIOPIA
SOMALIA
CENTRAL
CAN REPUBLIC
River Nile
River Zaire
Lake Turkana
MOGADISHU
UGANDA
KAMPALA
KENYA
Giraffe
ZAIRE
Lake Victoria
KIGALI
RWANDA
NAIROBI
Mount Kilimanjaro
ZAVILLE
BUJUMBURA
BURUNDI
HASA
TANZANIA
Lake Tanganyika
DODOMA
Dar es Salaam
Gorilla
Lake Nyasa
Comoro Islands
NGOLA
MALAWI
ZAMBIA
LILONGWE
LUSAKA
Zambezi River
MOZAMBIQUE
MADAGASCAR
HARARE
ZIMBABWE
ANTANANARIVO
Indian Ocean
MIBIA
HOEK
BOTSWANA
GABORONE
PRETORIA
Johannesburg
MAPUTO
SWAZILAND
MBABANE
Orange River
LESOTHO
MASERU
Drakensberg Mountains
SOUTH AFRICA
Durban
Cape Town
Clown anemone fish
N
NW
NE
W
E
SW
SE
S
2000
2500
3000
3500
2500
3000
3500
4000
4500
5000

United States of America

The USA is so wide that it crosses eight time zones.

When it is afternoon in New York, it is morning in Hawaii.

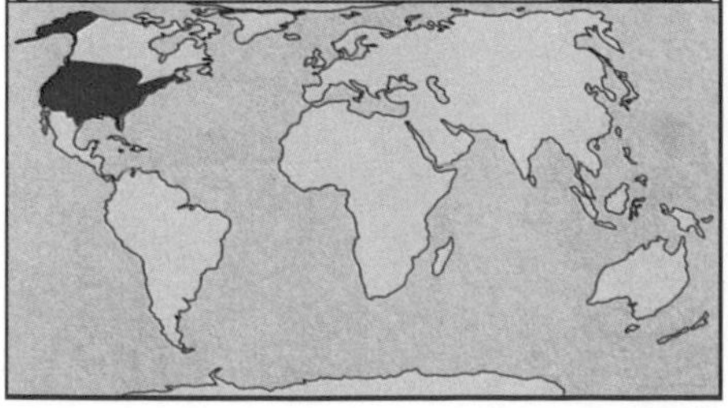

The huge Boeing factory in Seattle makes many of the world's airliners.
Alaska
JUNEAU
Seattle
OLYMPIA
Washington
SALEM
Redwoods
Oregon
HELENA
Grizzly bear
Montana
North Dak
BISM
BOISE
Idaho
Rocky Mountains
Puma
Wyoming
CHEYENNE
PIER
South Dak
Nebrask
Wine
CARSON CITY
SACRAMENTO
San Francisco
Nevada
SALT LAKE CITY
Utah
DENVER
Colorado
LIN
Kans
Rattlesnake
Surfer
California
Los Angeles
Grand Canyon
Arizona
PHOENIX
SANTA FE
New Mexico
Gila monster
Oklah
OKLA
Texas
The Alamo
AUS
Hawaii
HONOLULU
Gulf of California
Zuni corn dancer, Hopi tribe, New Mexico
MEXICO
MILES 250 500 1000
KILOMETRES 250 500 1000 1500 2000

Highest mountain: Mount McKinley, Alaska, 6,194 m.

Longest river: Mississippi-Missouri, 6,230 km.

Weather: The USA is so big that the weather ranges from very hot to very cold.

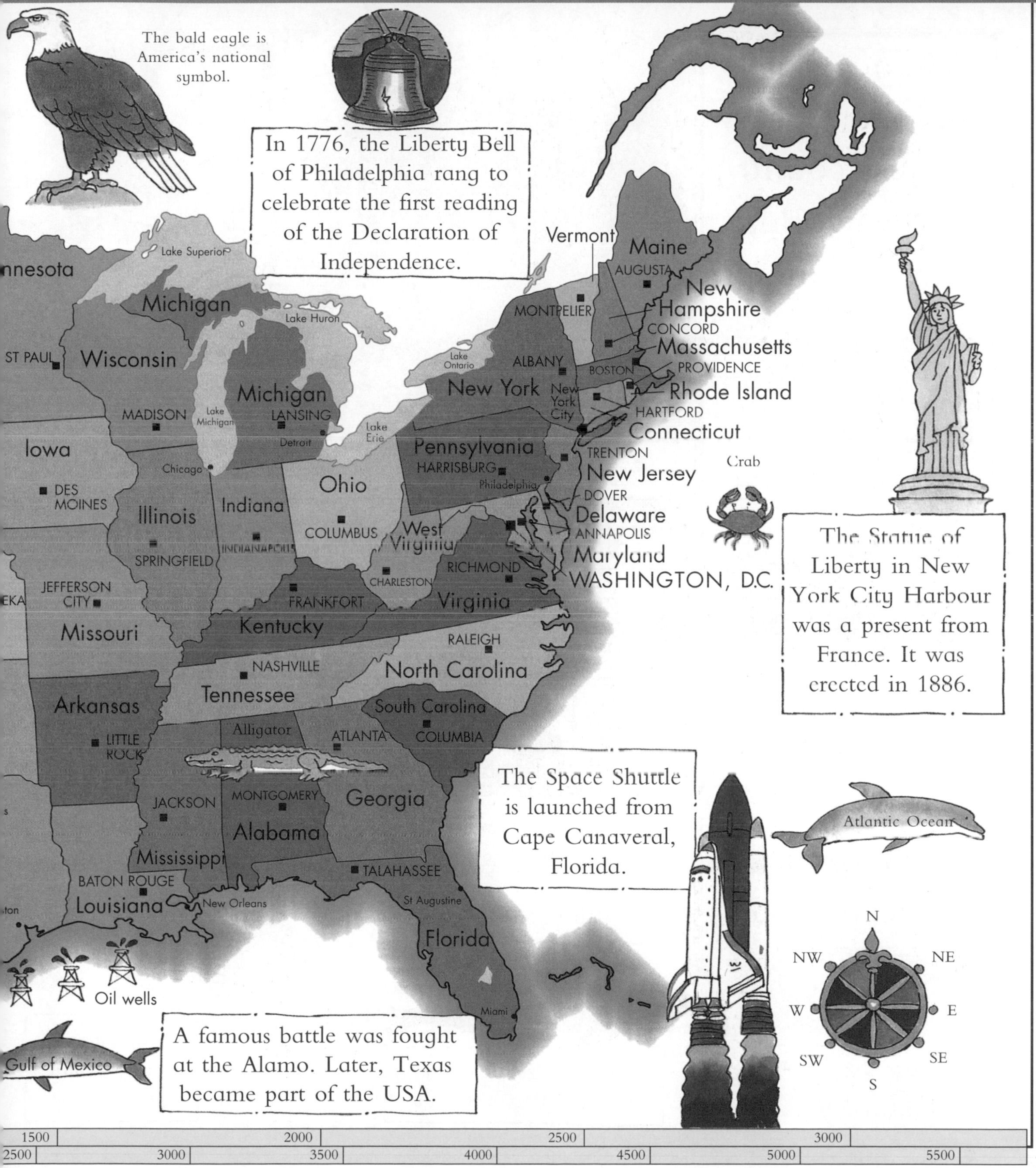

The bald eagle is America's national symbol.
In 1776, the Liberty Bell of Philadelphia rang to celebrate the first reading of the Declaration of Independence.
The Statue of Liberty in New York City Harbour was a present from France. It was erected in 1886.
The Space Shuttle is launched from Cape Canaveral, Florida.
A famous battle was fought at the Alamo. Later, Texas became part of the USA.
Lake Superior
nnesota
Michigan
Lake Huron
Lake Ontario
Lake Michigan
Lake Erie
ST PAUL
Wisconsin
MADISON
Michigan
LANSING
Detroit
Iowa
Chicago
DES MOINES
Illinois
SPRINGFIELD
Indiana
INDIANAPOLIS
Ohio
COLUMBUS
West Virginia
CHARLESTON
Pennsylvania
HARRISBURG
Philadelphia
New York
ALBANY
New York City
Vermont
MONTPELIER
Maine
AUGUSTA
New Hampshire
CONCORD
Massachusetts
BOSTON
PROVIDENCE
Rhode Island
HARTFORD
Connecticut
TRENTON
New Jersey
DOVER
Delaware
ANNAPOLIS
Maryland
WASHINGTON, D.C.
Crab
RICHMOND
Virginia
FRANKFORT
Kentucky
JEFFERSON CITY
EKA
Missouri
RALEIGH
North Carolina
NASHVILLE
Tennessee
Arkansas
LITTLE ROCK
South Carolina
COLUMBIA
Alligator
ATLANTA
JACKSON
MONTGOMERY
Georgia
Alabama
Mississippi
TALAHASSEE
BATON ROUGE
Louisiana
New Orleans
St Augustine
Florida
Miami
Oil wells
Gulf of Mexico
Atlantic Ocean
N
NE
E
SE
S
SW
W
NW
1500
2000
2500
3000
2500
3000
3500
4000
4500
5000
5500

CANADA

Highest mountain:
Mount Logan,
5,951 m.

Longest river:
Mackenzie,
4,241 km.

Canada is the second largest country in the world, but has only one ninth of the population of the USA.

Most people prefer to live in the south, rather than the Arctic north.

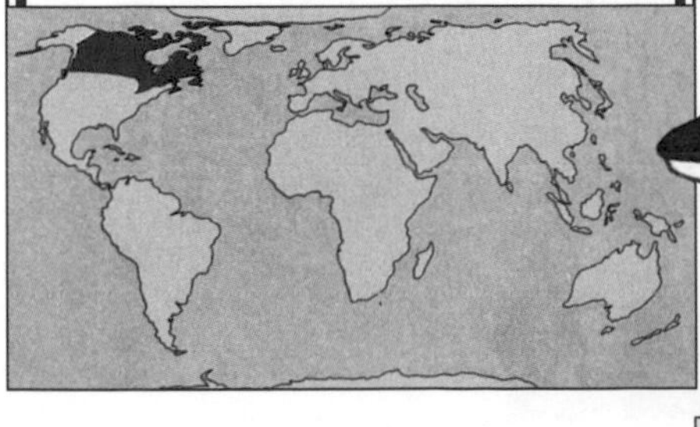

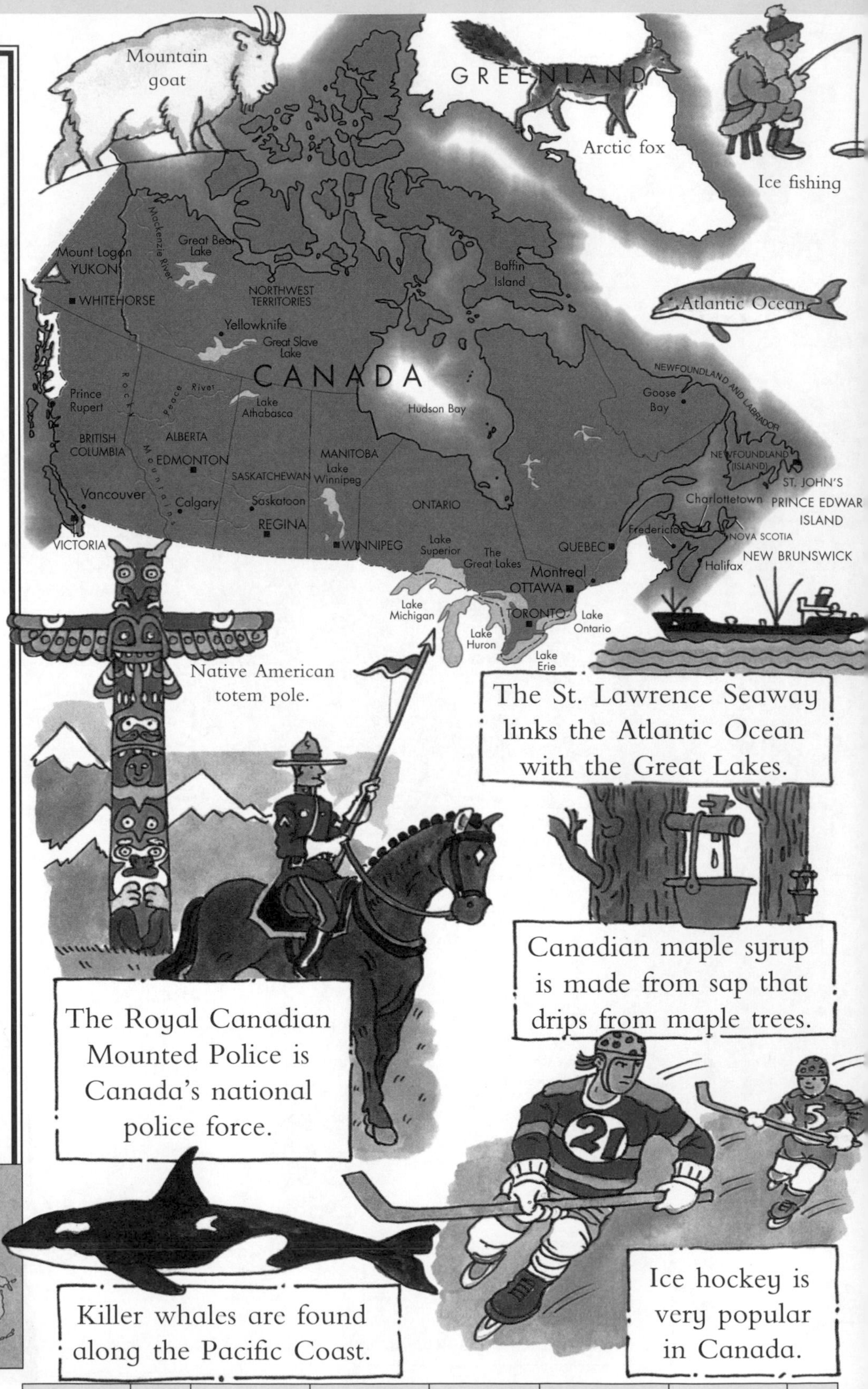

Mountain goat
GREENLAND
Arctic fox
Ice fishing
Atlantic Ocean
Mount Logan
YUKON
Mackenzie River
Great Bear Lake
WHITEHORSE
NORTHWEST TERRITORIES
Baffin Island
Yellowknife
Great Slave Lake
CANADA
Rocky Mountains
Peace River
Prince Rupert
Lake Athabasca
Hudson Bay
NEWFOUNDLAND AND LABRADOR
Goose Bay
BRITISH COLUMBIA
ALBERTA
EDMONTON
MANITOBA
Lake Winnipeg
SASKATCHEWAN
NEWFOUNDLAND (ISLAND)
ST. JOHN'S
Vancouver
Calgary
Saskatoon
ONTARIO
Charlottetown
PRINCE EDWARD ISLAND
REGINA
Fredericton
NOVA SCOTIA
VICTORIA
WINNIPEG
Lake Superior
The Great Lakes
QUEBEC
Halifax
NEW BRUNSWICK
Montreal
OTTAWA
Lake Michigan
TORONTO
Lake Ontario
Lake Huron
Lake Erie
Native American totem pole.

The St. Lawrence Seaway links the Atlantic Ocean with the Great Lakes.

Canadian maple syrup is made from sap that drips from maple trees.

The Royal Canadian Mounted Police is Canada's national police force.

Killer whales are found along the Pacific Coast.

Ice hockey is very popular in Canada.

MILES 250	500	1000	1500	2000	2500	3000				
KILOMETRES	1000	1500	2000	2500	3000	3500	4000	4500	5000	

Central America

Highest mountain:
Mount Orizaba,
5,700 m.

Mexico and Central America link the USA and South America.

Mexico is the largest country in this region. Much of the country is very high, dry and rocky.

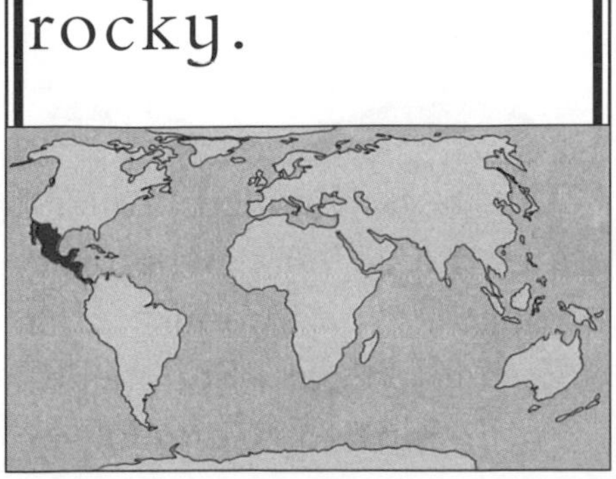

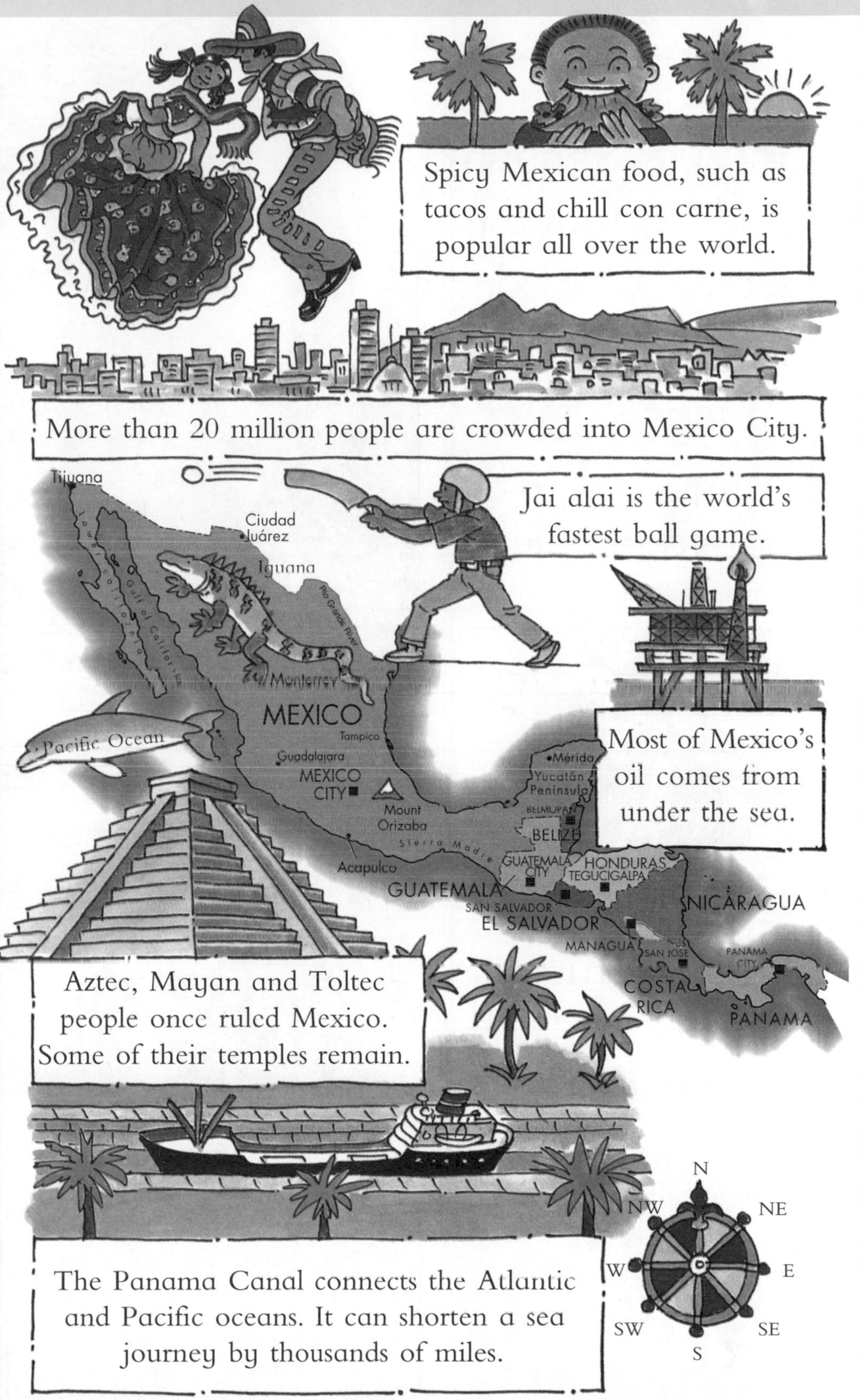

Tijuana
Ciudad Juárez
Iguana
Gulf of California
Rio Grande River
Monterrey
MEXICO
Tampico
Pacific Ocean
Guadalajara
MEXICO CITY
Mount Orizaba
Mérida
Yucatán Peninsula
BELMOPAN
BELIZE
Sierra Madre
Acapulco
GUATEMALA CITY
HONDURAS
TEGUCIGALPA
GUATEMALA
SAN SALVADOR
EL SALVADOR
NICARAGUA
MANAGUA
SAN JOSE
PANAMA CITY
COSTA RICA
PANAMA
N
NE
E
SE
S
SW
W
NW

Spicy Mexican food, such as tacos and chill con carne, is popular all over the world.

More than 20 million people are crowded into Mexico City.

Jai alai is the world's fastest ball game.

Most of Mexico's oil comes from under the sea.

Aztec, Mayan and Toltec people once ruled Mexico. Some of their temples remain.

The Panama Canal connects the Atlantic and Pacific oceans. It can shorten a sea journey by thousands of miles.

Miles	250	500	1000	1500	2000		
Kilometres	500	1000	1500	2000	2500	3000	3500

SOUTH AMERICA

In the early 1500s, Spanish and Portuguese settlers arrived in South America. They conquered the native people.

Now, a mix of Indians, Africans and Europeans live there.

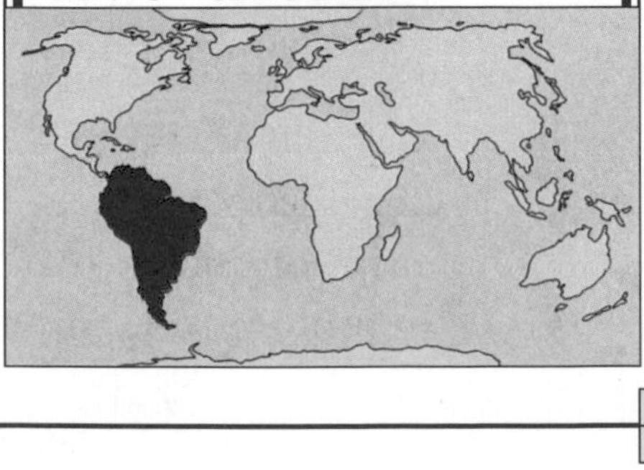

Giant tortoises live on the Galápagos Islands.

Rivers and streams feed into the mighty Amazon River from an area ten times as big as France. This area is called the Amazon Basin and covers parts of Brazil, Peru and Colombia.

This area has more species of living things than anywhere else in the world. There are over 50,000 types of plants!

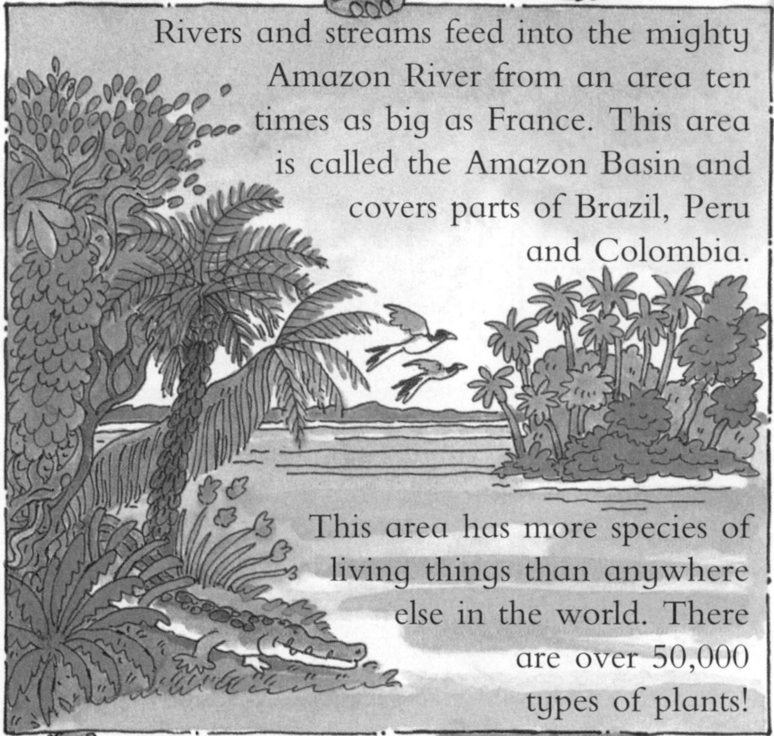

Andean cock-of-the-rock

Farmers, lumberjacks and miners clear huge areas of rainforest every day. Without trees, the soil is soon washed away by heavy rain, leaving barren ground where nothing grows.

The capybara, a relative of the guinea pig, is the world's largest rodent. It is over a metre long!

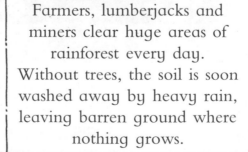

MILES	250	500	1000	1500	2000	2500			
KILOMETRES	500	1000	1500	2000	2500	3000	3500	4000	

Highest mountain: Mount Aconcagua. Argentina, 6,960 m.

Longest river: Amazon River, 6,437 km.

Weather: It is cold in the Andes and the far south, but very hot and humid in the rainforests.

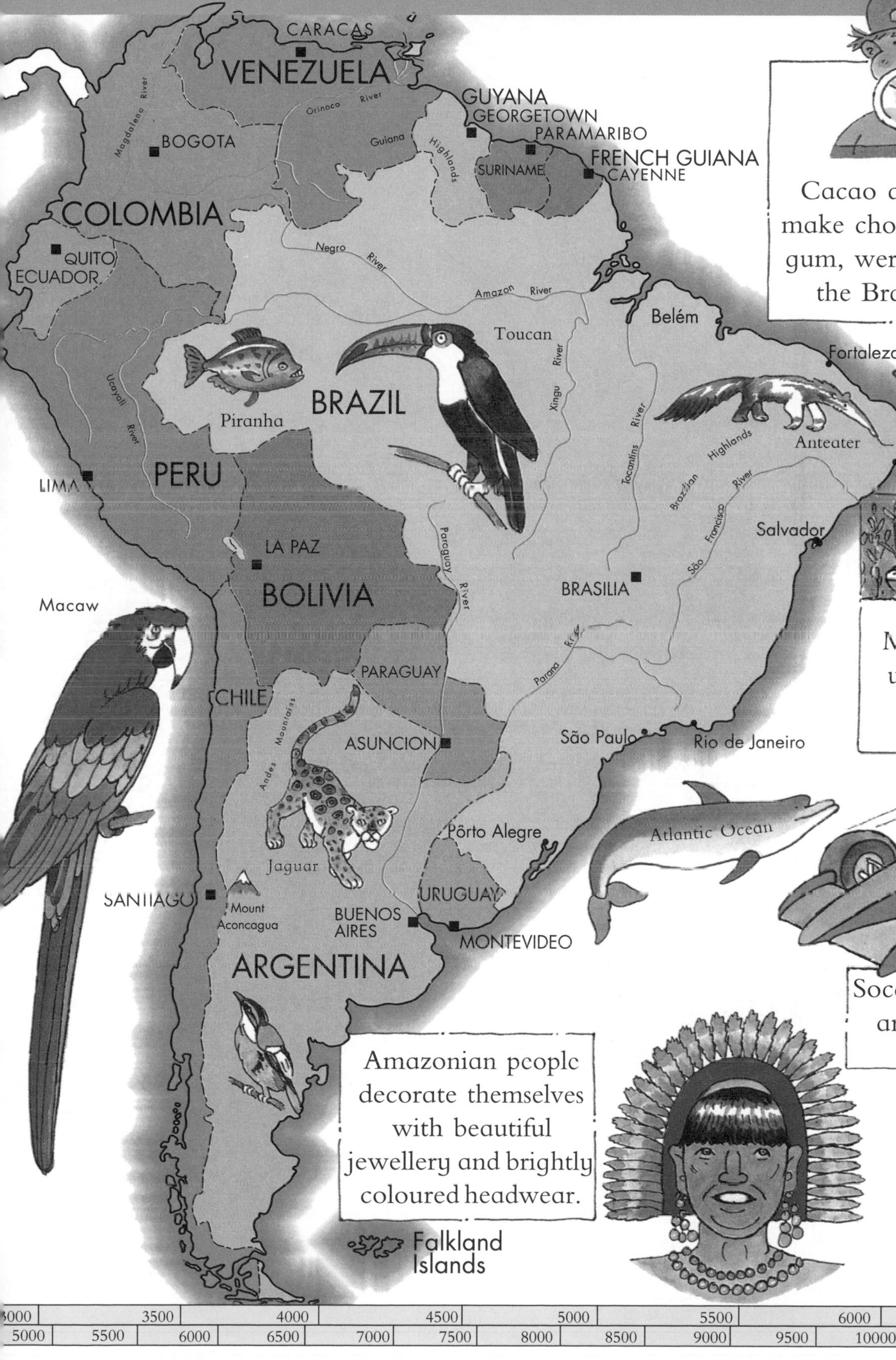

CARACAS
VENEZUELA
Orinoco River
Magdalena River
BOGOTA
COLOMBIA
Guiana Highlands
GUYANA
GEORGETOWN
PARAMARIBO
SURINAME
FRENCH GUIANA
CAYENNE
QUITO
ECUADOR
Negro River
Amazon River
Belém
Fortaleza
Toucan
Xingu River
Piranha
BRAZIL
Ucayali River
Tocantins River
Brazilian Highlands
Anteater
Atlantic Ocean
Recife
LIMA
PERU
São Francisco River
Salvador
LA PAZ
BOLIVIA
Paraguay River
BRASILIA
Macaw
Parana River
PARAGUAY
CHILE
Andes Mountains
ASUNCION
São Paulo
Rio de Janeiro
Atlantic Ocean
Pôrto Alegre
Jaguar
SANTIAGO
Mount Aconcagua
BUENOS AIRES
URUGUAY
MONTEVIDEO
ARGENTINA
Falkland Islands
3000 3500 4000 4500 5000 5500 6000 6500 7000
5000 5500 6000 6500 7000 7500 8000 8500 9000 9500 10000 10500 11000 11500

Cacao and chicle, used to make chocolate and chewing gum, were first discovered in the Brazilian rainforest.

Many cars in Brazil use fuel made from sugar cane.

Soccer and auto racing are very popular in South America.

Amazonian people decorate themselves with beautiful jewellery and brightly coloured headwear.

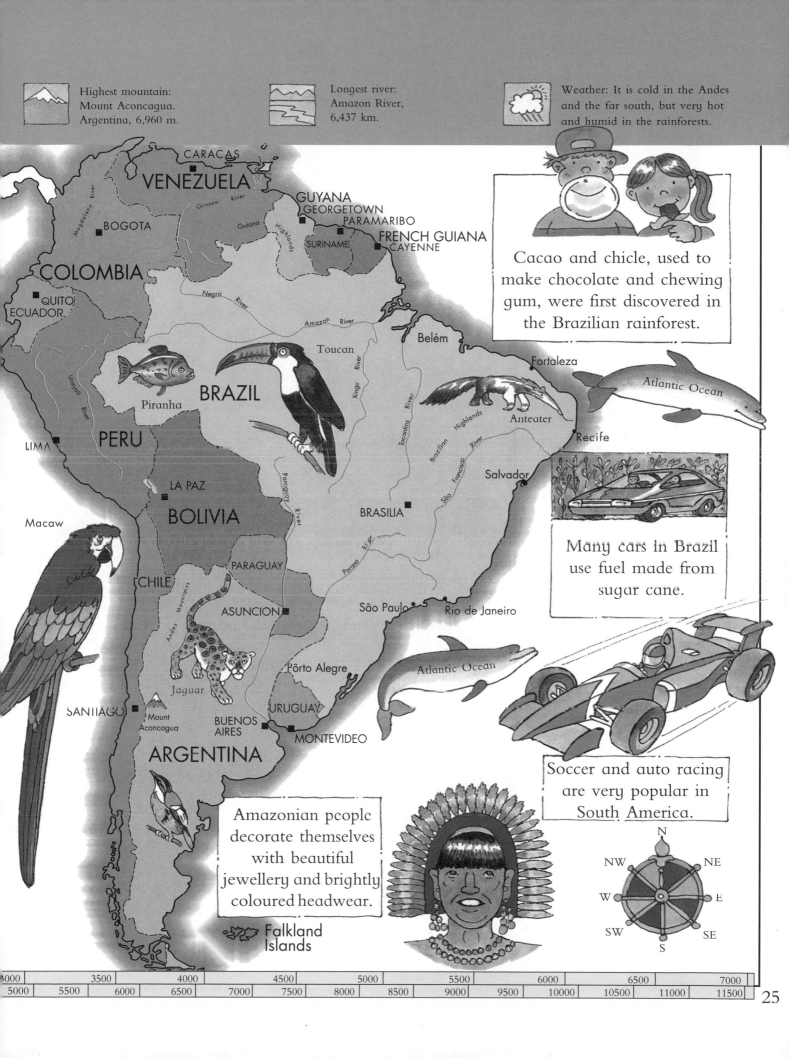

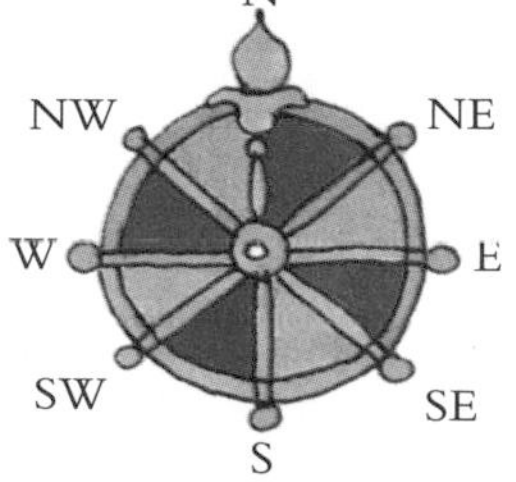

N
NW
NE
W
E
SW
SE
S

The Middle East

Most of the Middle East is covered with desert and mountains.

There is lots of valuable oil under the desert and seabed. Oil is sold to other countries to use as fuel.

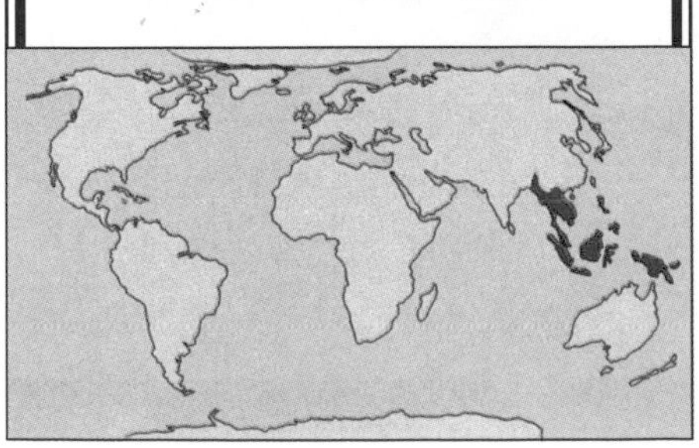

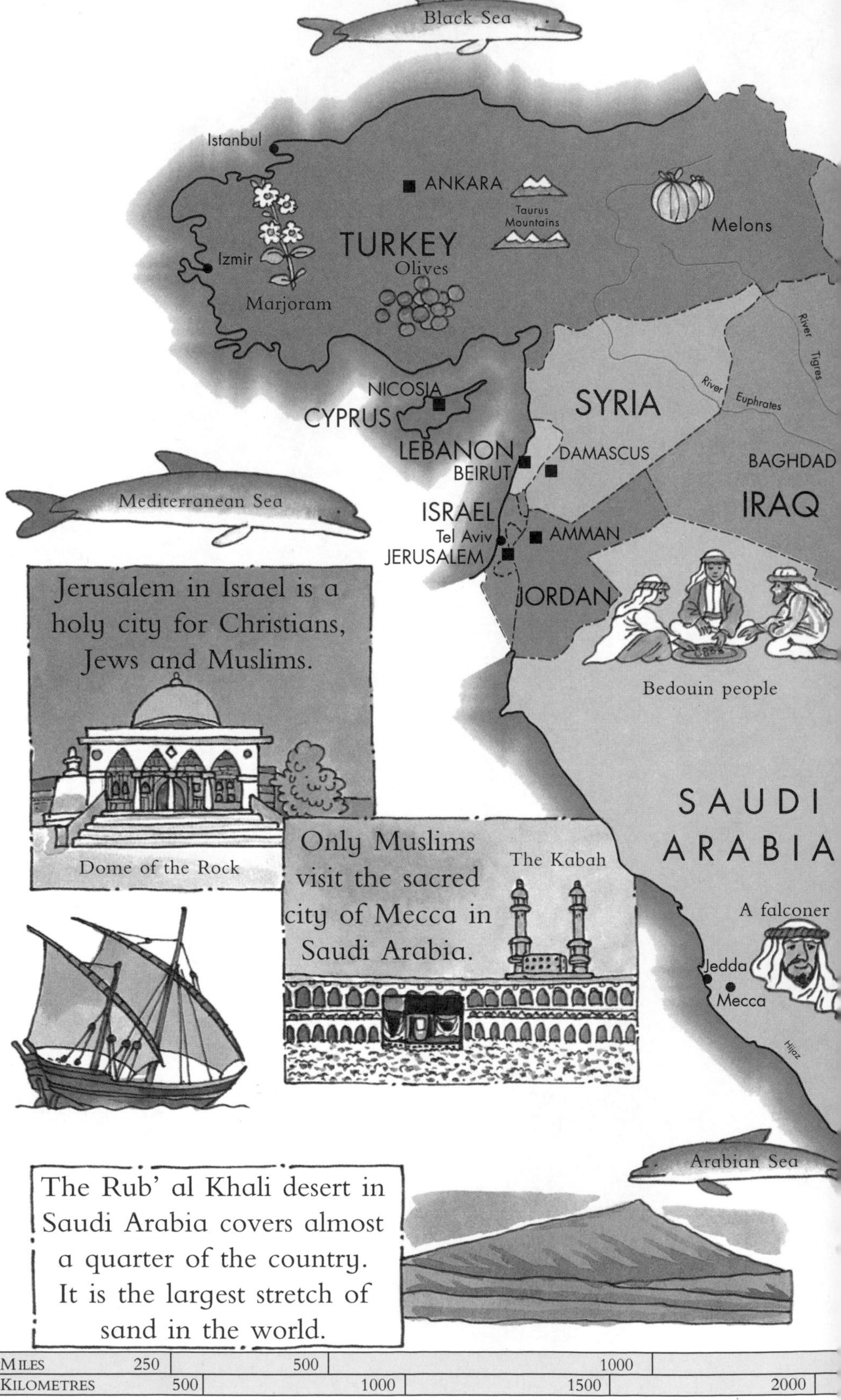

Black Sea
Istanbul
ANKARA
Taurus Mountains
Melons
TURKEY
Izmir
Olives
Marjoram
River Tigres
River Euphrates
NICOSIA
CYPRUS
SYRIA
LEBANON
DAMASCUS
BEIRUT
BAGHDAD
Mediterranean Sea
IRAQ
ISRAEL
Tel Aviv
AMMAN
JERUSALEM
JORDAN
Jerusalem in Israel is a holy city for Christians, Jews and Muslims.
Bedouin people
Dome of the Rock
SAUDI ARABIA
Only Muslims visit the sacred city of Mecca in Saudi Arabia.
The Kabah
A falconer
Jedda
Mecca
Hijaz
Arabian Sea
The Rub' al Khali desert in Saudi Arabia covers almost a quarter of the country. It is the largest stretch of sand in the world.
MILES 250 500 1000
KILOMETRES 500 1000 1500 2000

Highest mountain: Elbruz Mountains, Iran, 5,600 m.

Longest river: Euphrates, 2,740 km.

Weather: These countries have hot, dry summers but in the north, the winters are often cold.

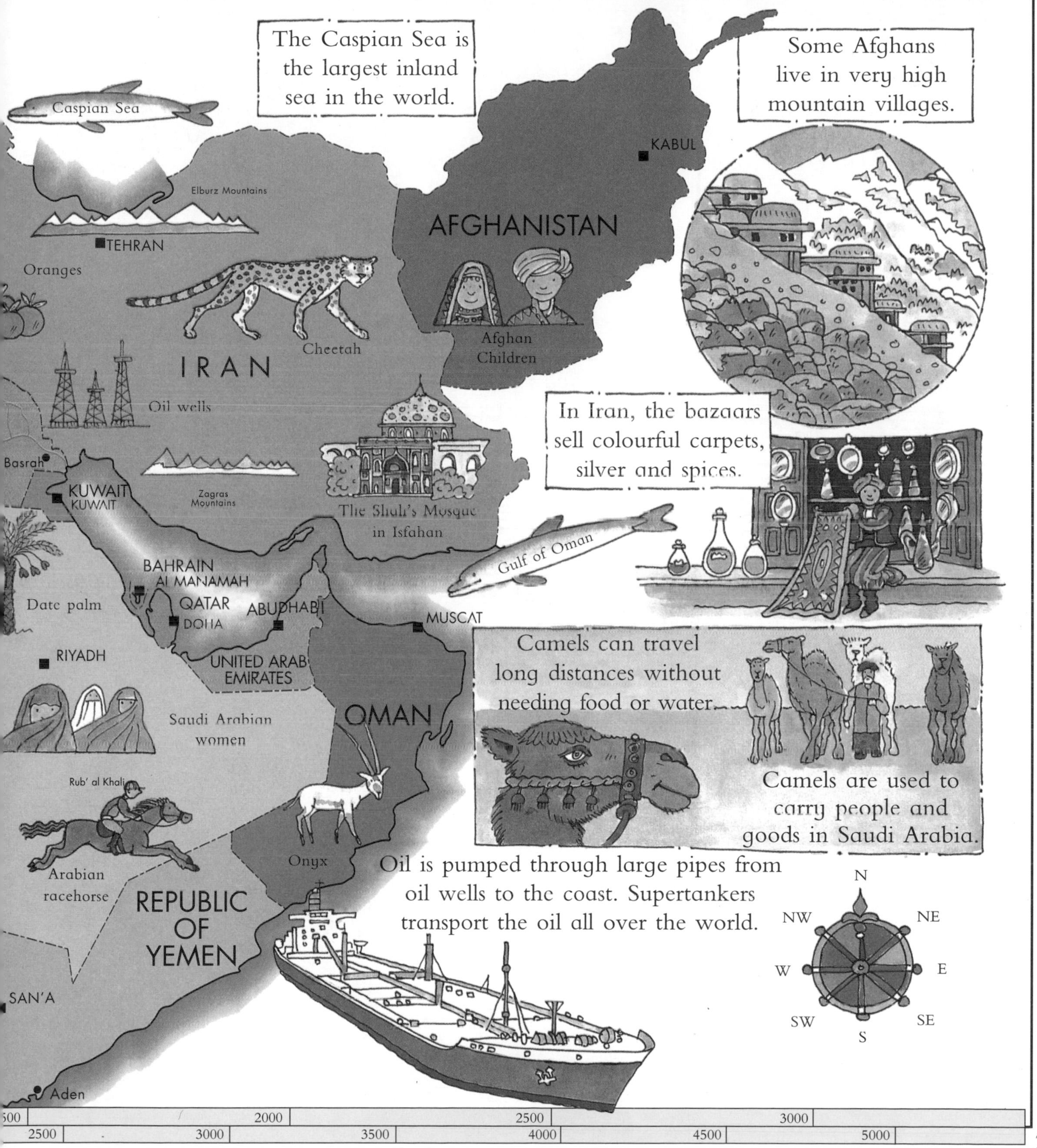

Caspian Sea
Elburz Mountains
TEHRAN
Oranges
Cheetah
IRAN
Oil wells
Basrah
KUWAIT
KUWAIT
Zagros Mountains
The Shah's Mosque in Isfahan
AFGHANISTAN
KABUL
Afghan Children
Gulf of Oman
BAHRAIN
Al MANAMAH
QATAR
DOHA
ABU DHABI
UNITED ARAB EMIRATES
MUSCAT
Date palm
RIYADH
Saudi Arabian women
OMAN
Rub' al Khali
Arabian racehorse
Onyx
REPUBLIC OF YEMEN
SAN'A
Aden
N
NE
E
SE
S
SW
W
NW
500
2000
2500
3000
2500
3000
3500
4000
4500
5000

The Caspian Sea is the largest inland sea in the world.

Some Afghans live in very high mountain villages.

In Iran, the bazaars sell colourful carpets, silver and spices.

Camels can travel long distances without needing food or water.

Camels are used to carry people and goods in Saudi Arabia.

Oil is pumped through large pipes from oil wells to the coast. Supertankers transport the oil all over the world.

SOUTHERN ASIA

Asian farmers rely on the important monsoon rains to make their crops grow.

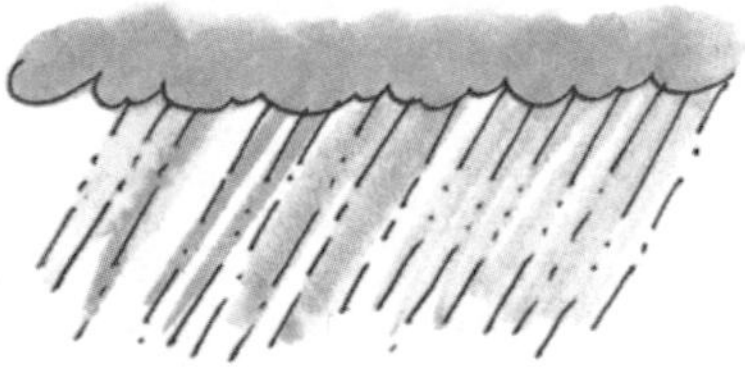

If there is too much rain, floods can destroy crops and villages.

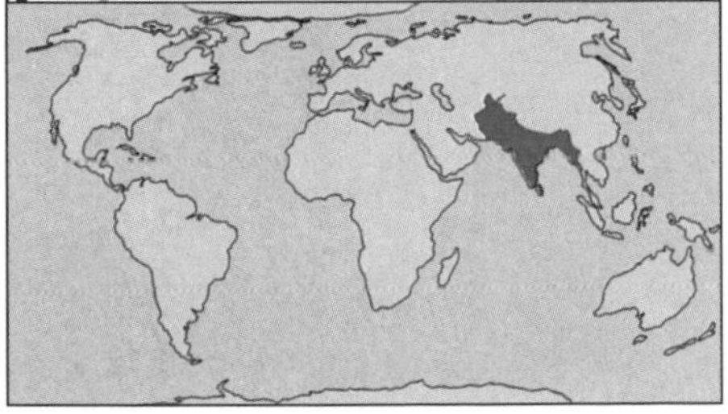

One-fifth of Afghanistan's people are nomads. They wander from place to place.

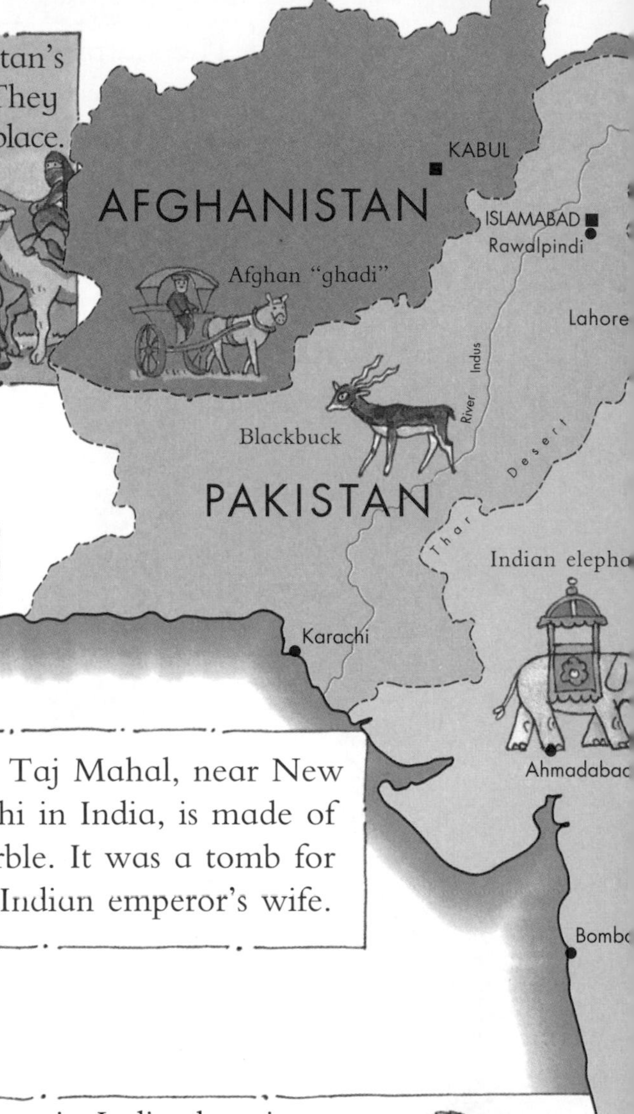

Pakistan's official language is Urdu.

The Taj Mahal, near New Delhi in India, is made of marble. It was a tomb for an Indian emperor's wife.

More tea is grown in India than in any other country in the world.

Leaves from tea plants are picked, dried and crushed into tea leaves.

MILES	250	500	1000	
KILOMETRES 250	500	1000	1500	2000

| Highest mountain: Mount Everest, 8,848 m. | Longest river: Bramahputra, 2,900 km. | Weather: It is mostly hot, but very cold in the mountains. |

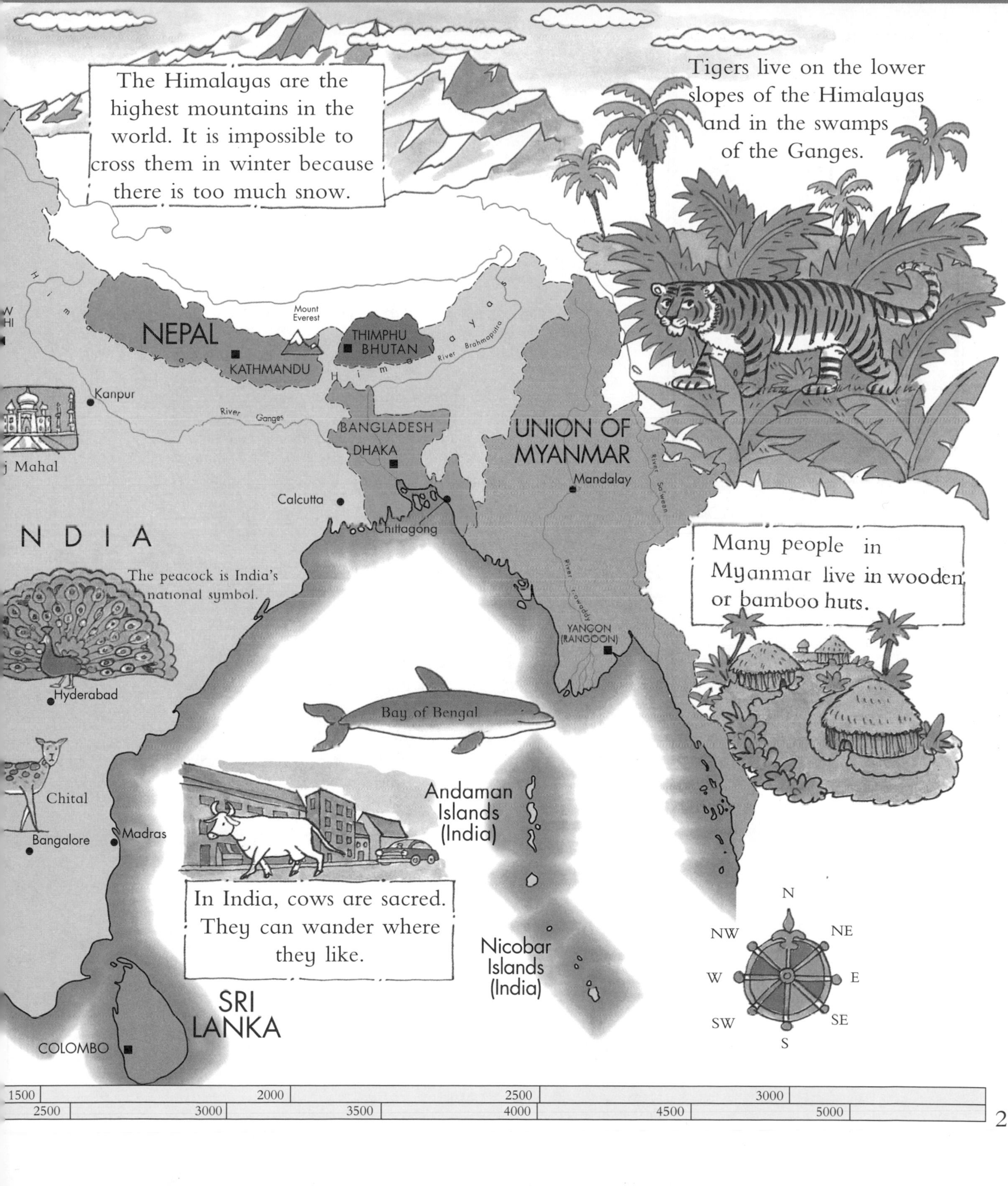

The Himalayas are the highest mountains in the world. It is impossible to cross them in winter because there is too much snow.

Tigers live on the lower slopes of the Himalayas and in the swamps of the Ganges.

W HI

Hi malaya

NEPAL

Mount Everest

KATHMANDU

THIMPHU
BHUTAN

alaya

Hima laya

River Brahmaputra

Kanpur

River   Ganges

BANGLADESH

DHAKA

UNION OF
MYANMAR

Mandalay

River Salween

Calcutta

Chittagong

N D I A

The peacock is India's national symbol.

j Mahal

River Irrawaddy

Many people in Myanmar live in wooden or bamboo huts.

Hyderabad

YANGON
(RANGOON)

Bay of Bengal

Chital

Andaman
Islands
(India)

Bangalore

Madras

In India, cows are sacred. They can wander where they like.

Nicobar
Islands
(India)

N

NW   NE

W   E

SW   SE

S

SRI
LANKA

COLOMBO

| 1500 | | 2000 | | 2500 | | 3000 | |
| 2500 | 3000 | 3500 | 4000 | 4500 | 5000 |

SOUTHEAST ASIA AND PACIFIC

The Pacific Islands curve from Southeast Asia towards Australia.

There are thousands of islands. Some are volcanic.

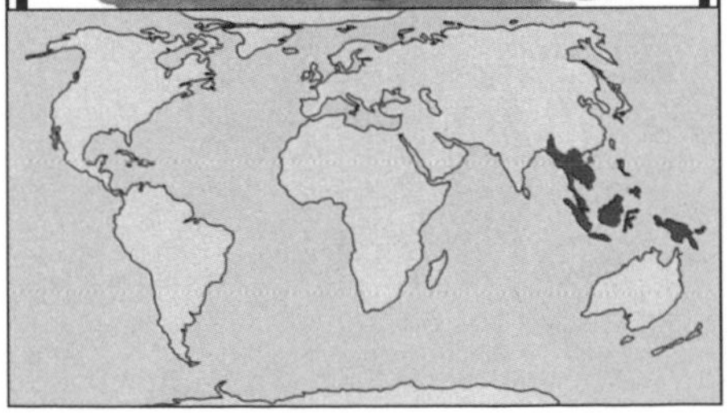

Tigers, rhinoceros, water buffalo and elephants are all found in Southeast Asia.

Many islands are made of coral. It takes millions of sea creatures' skeletons to form one small coral island.

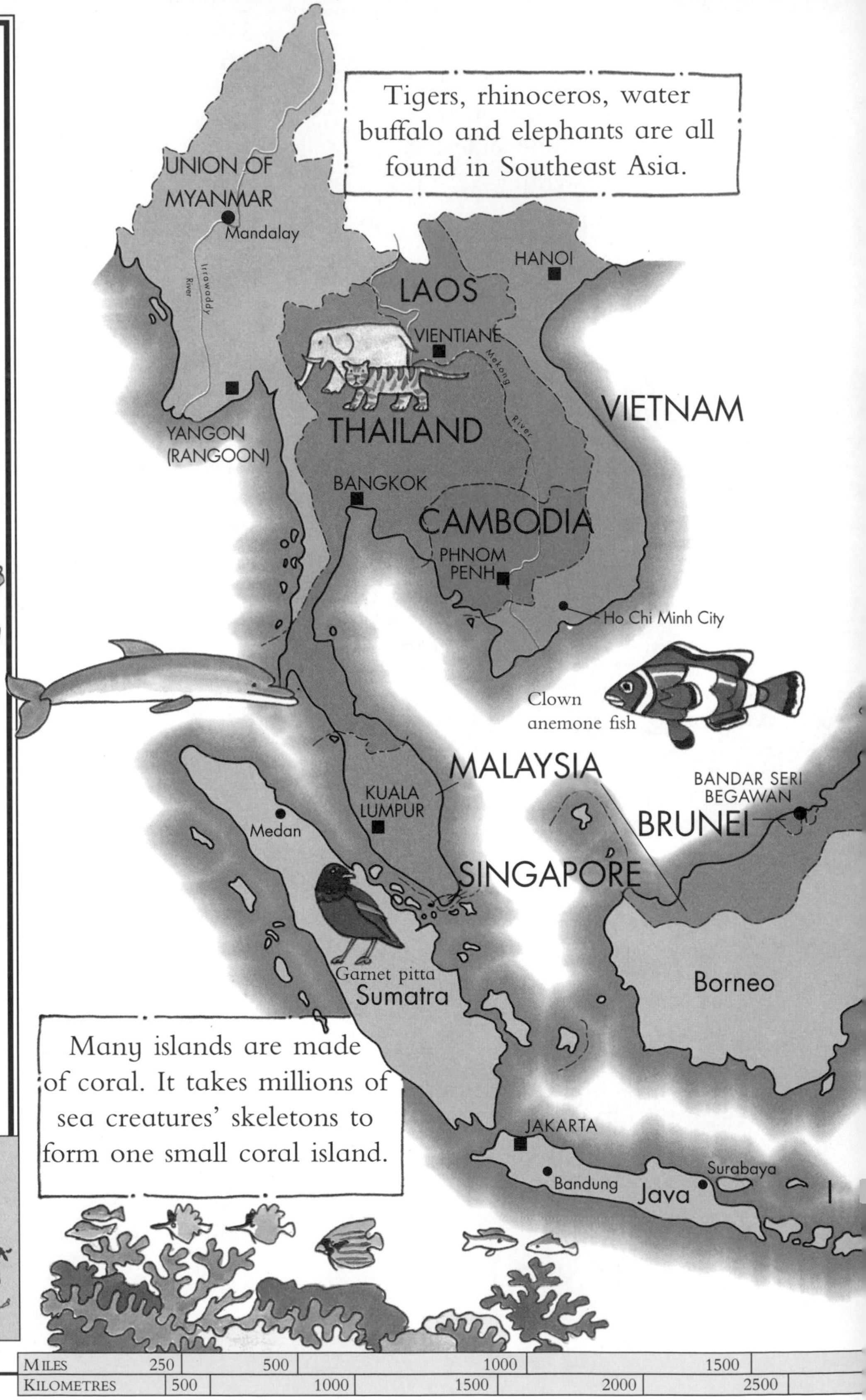

UNION OF MYANMAR
Mandalay
Irrawaddy River
YANGON (RANGOON)
LAOS
HANOI
VIENTIANE
Mekong River
THAILAND
VIETNAM
BANGKOK
CAMBODIA
PHNOM PENH
Ho Chi Minh City
Clown anemone fish
MALAYSIA
KUALA LUMPUR
Medan
BANDAR SERI BEGAWAN
BRUNEI
SINGAPORE
Garnet pitta
Sumatra
Borneo
JAKARTA
Bandung
Java
Surabaya
MILES 250 500 1000 1500
KILOMETRES 500 1000 1500 2000 2500

ISLANDS

Highest mountain: Puncak Jaya, New Guinea, 5,030 m.

Longest river: Mekong River, 4,350 km.

Weather: It is warm all year, but the monsoon wind brings heavy rains.

Many islanders are fishermen. Their boats are like canoes with small sails.

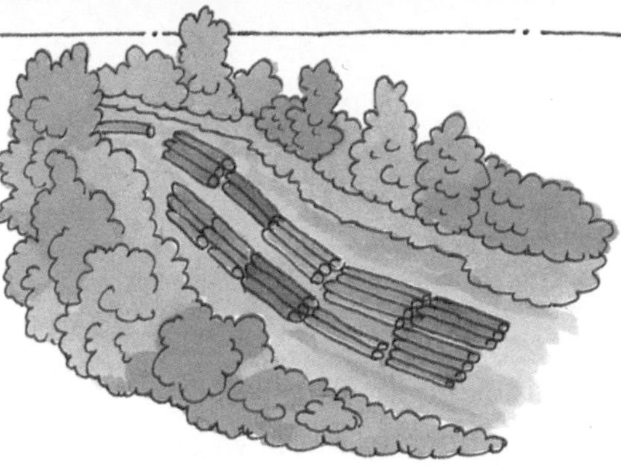

Timber is floated down rivers from forests to the sawmills.

Farmers grow many crops such as rice, maize, tea, coffee and spices.

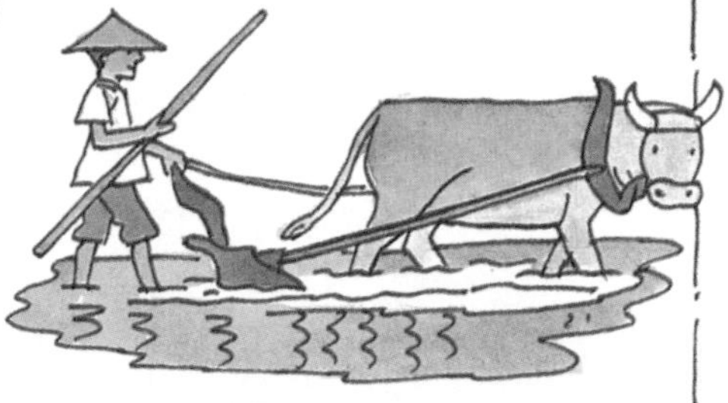

Hundreds of languages are spoken in Southeast Asia and many different religions are practised.

There are over 7,000 islands in the Philippines.

Wooden house on stilts

Papua New Guinea is nearly twice the size of Britain.

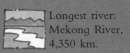

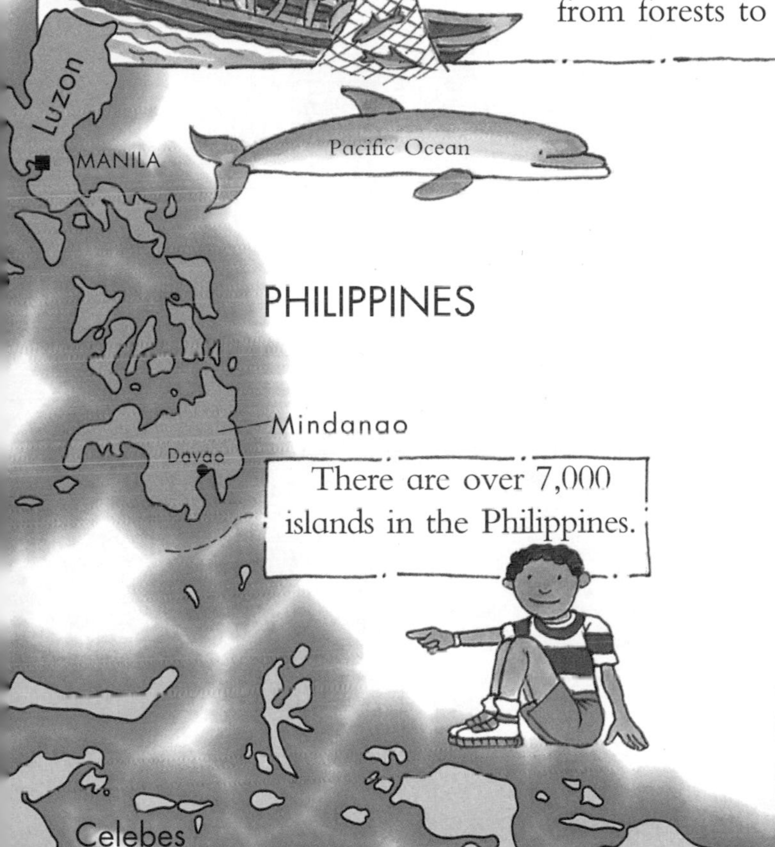
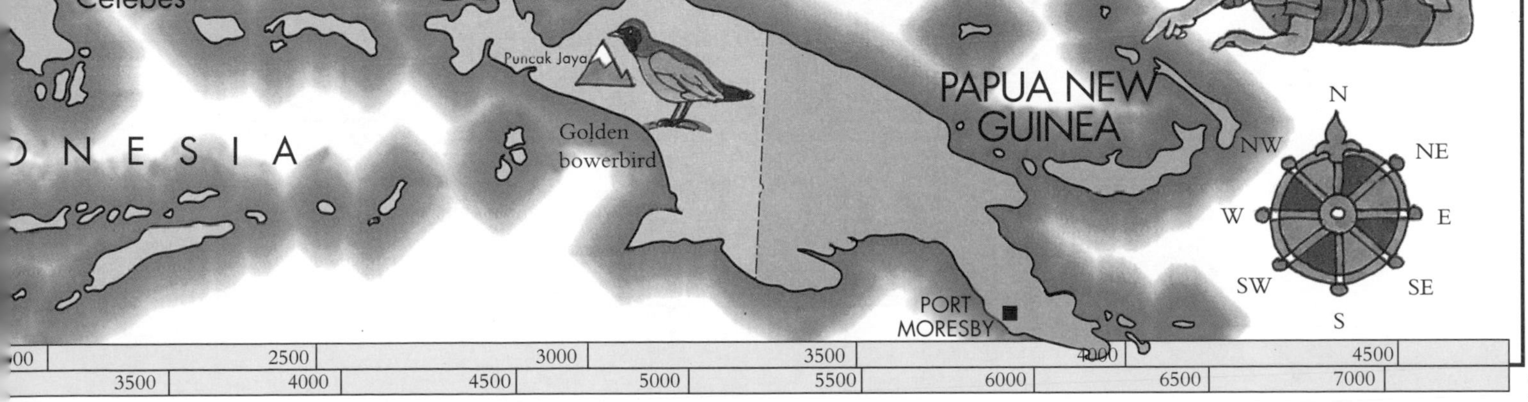

EAST ASIA

More people live in China than in any other country in the world.

Japan is made up of four large islands and thousands of small ones.

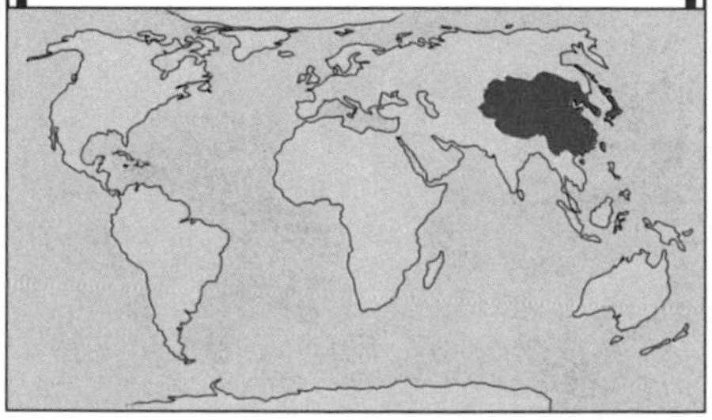

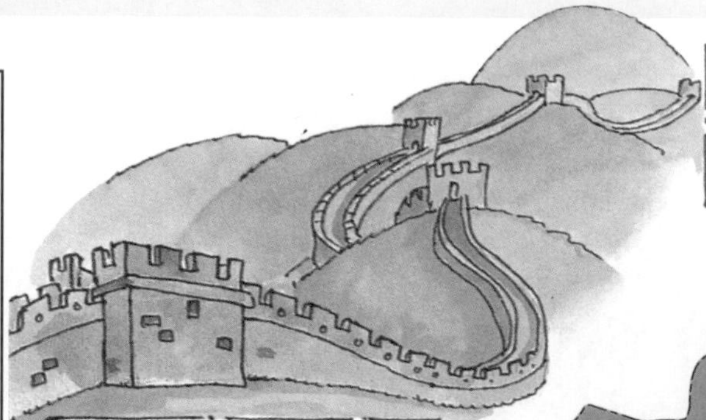

Mongolians are well known as expert horse riders.

The Great Wall of China was built to keep out enemies. It is 2,000 years old.

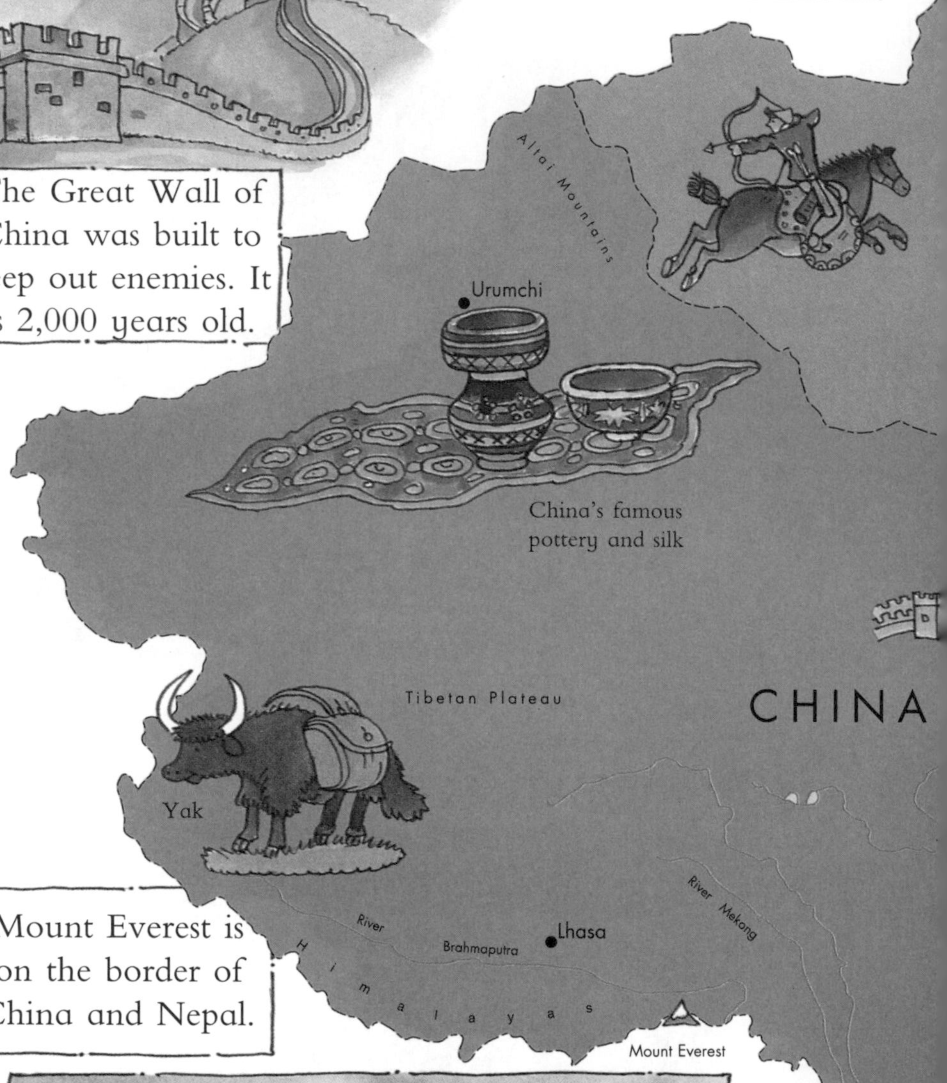

Mount Everest is on the border of China and Nepal.

China is the world's largest rice producer. The rice is planted in flooded fields known as paddies.

Miles	250	500	1000	
Kilometres 250	500	1000	1500	2000

Highest mountain:
Mount Everest,
China/Nepal, 8,848m.

Longest river:
Chang Jiang,
China, 5,530km.

Weather: The north has wet summers and dry winters. The south is hot all year.

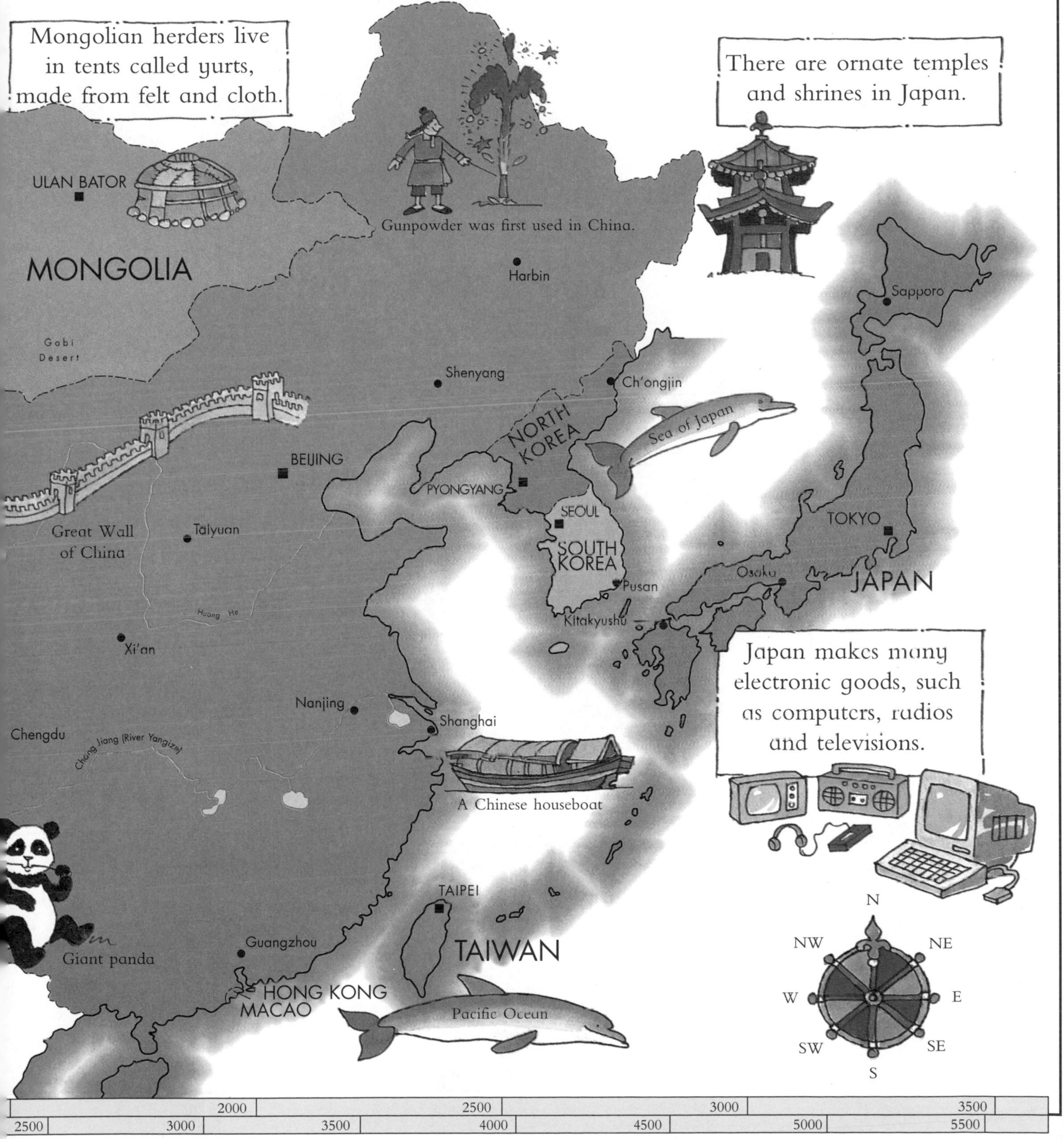

Mongolian herders live in tents called yurts, made from felt and cloth.
Gunpowder was first used in China.
There are ornate temples and shrines in Japan.
ULAN BATOR
MONGOLIA
Harbin
Sapporo
Gobi Desert
Shenyang
Ch'ongjin
Sea of Japan
NORTH KOREA
BEIJING
PYONGYANG
SEOUL
SOUTH KOREA
TOKYO
Great Wall of China
Taiyuan
Pusan
Osaka
JAPAN
Huang He
Kitakyushu
Xi'an
Japan makes many electronic goods, such as computers, radios and televisions.
Nanjing
Shanghai
Chengdu
Chang Jiang (River Yangize)
A Chinese houseboat
TAIPEI
TAIWAN
Guangzhou
Giant panda
HONG KONG
MACAO
Pacific Ocean
N
NW
NE
W
E
SW
SE
S
2000
2500
3000
3500
2500
3000
3500
4000
4500
5000
5500

AUSTRALIA AND NEW ZEALAND

A large part of Australia is very dry and barren. This is known as the 'outback'.

New Zealand is 1,529 kilometres southeast of Australia.

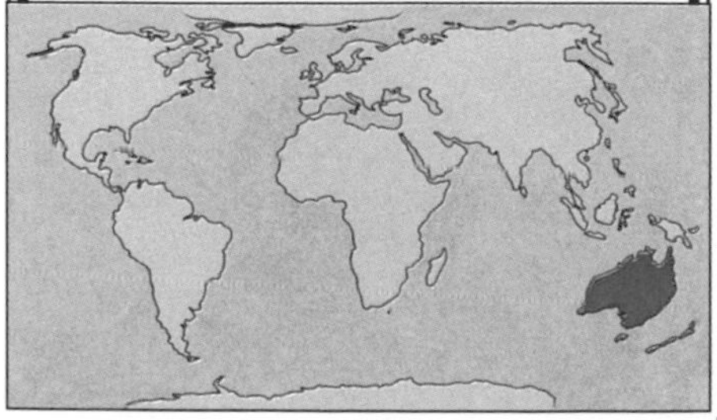

Australia has the world's largest wool industry. More sheep than people live here!

Australia's native people are called Aboriginals. They were the country's only inhabitants until about 200 years ago.

Aboriginal painting

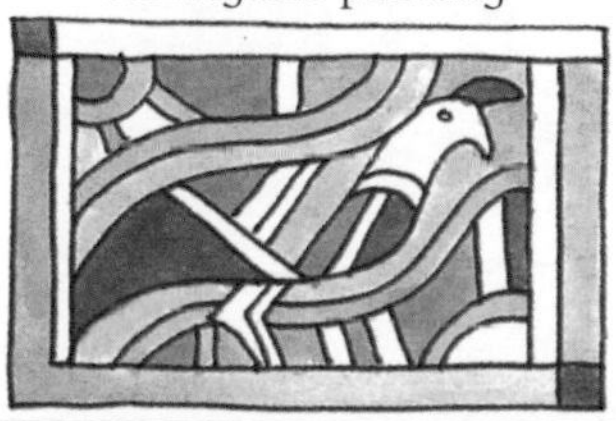

MILES	250	500		1000	
KILOMETRES	500		1000	1500	2000

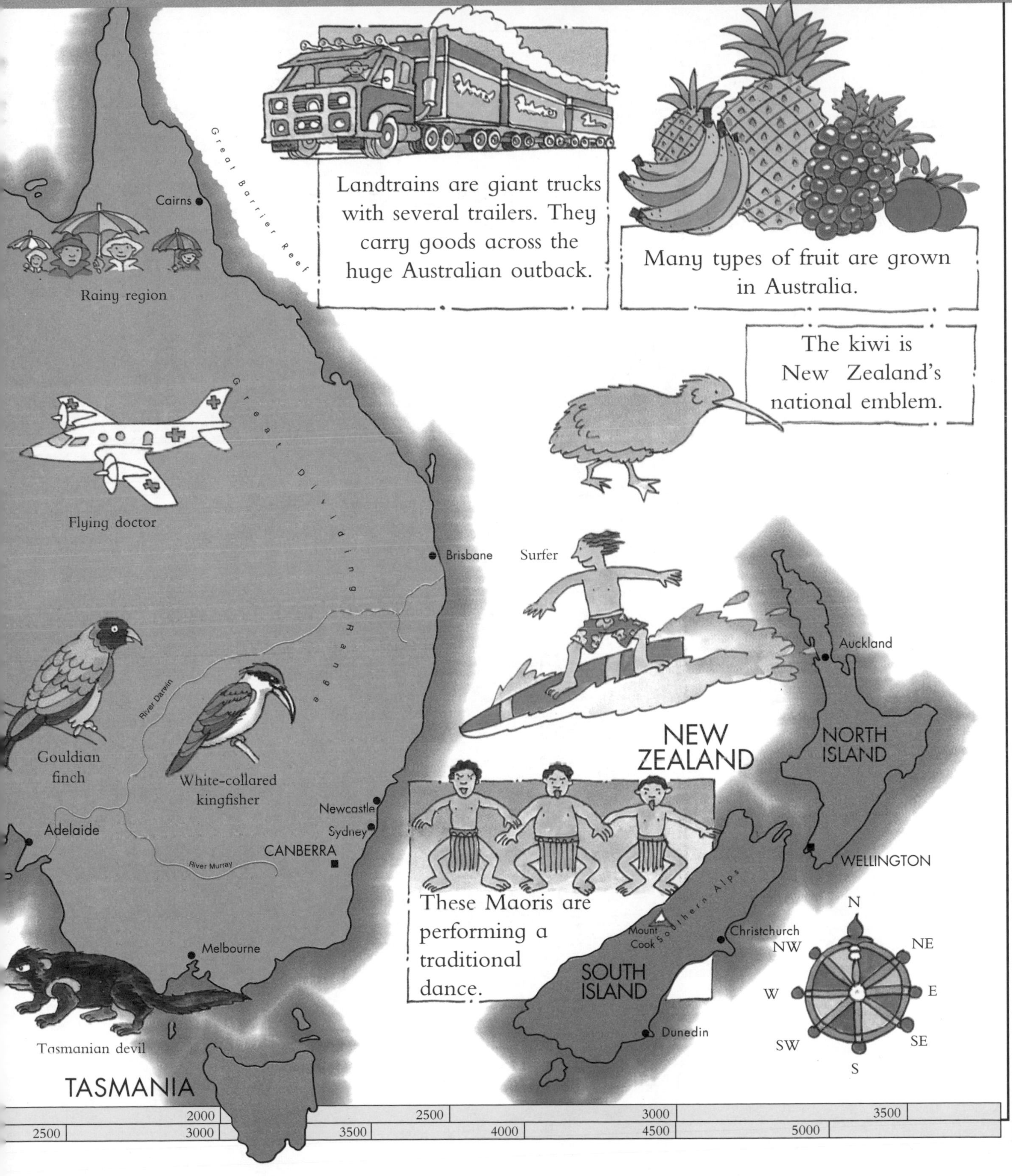
Highest mountain: Mount Cook, New Zealand, 3,764 m.
Longest river: Murray River, Australia, 2,589 km.
Weather: Most of Australia is dry and hot. It is wet in the eastern mountains and in New Zealand.
Landtrains are giant trucks with several trailers. They carry goods across the huge Australian outback.
Many types of fruit are grown in Australia.
The kiwi is New Zealand's national emblem.
Great Barrier Reef
Cairns
Raining region
Great Dividing Range
Flying doctor
Brisbane
Surfer
Auckland
NEW ZEALAND
NORTH ISLAND
River Darwin
Gouldian finch
White-collared kingfisher
Newcastle
Sydney
Adelaide
CANBERRA
River Murray
WELLINGTON
These Maoris are performing a traditional dance.
Southern Alps
Mount Cook
Christchurch
SOUTH ISLAND
N
NW
NE
W
E
SW
SE
S
Melbourne
Dunedin
Tasmanian devil
TASMANIA
2000
2500
3000
3500
2500
3000
3500
4000
4500
5000

ARCTIC

The Arctic is the area around the North Pole at the very top of the world. The Arctic Ocean is icy cold and much of it is frozen solid for most of the year.

In 1909, an American called Robert Peary used dog sleds to become the first person to reach the North Pole.

Yukon River
Snowy owl
ALASKA (USA)
River Kolyma
River Indigirka
Puffin
River Lena
CANADA
Arctic fox
Arctic Ocean
North Pole
RUSSIA
Yenisey River
GREENLAND
River Ob
River Pechora
Snow bunting
Godthab
Murmansk
REYKJAVIK
Arctic Circle
ICELAND
NORWAY
SWEDEN
FINLAND
HELSINKI
OSLO
STOCKHOLM
SCOTLAND
DENMARK
Lemming

Polar bear

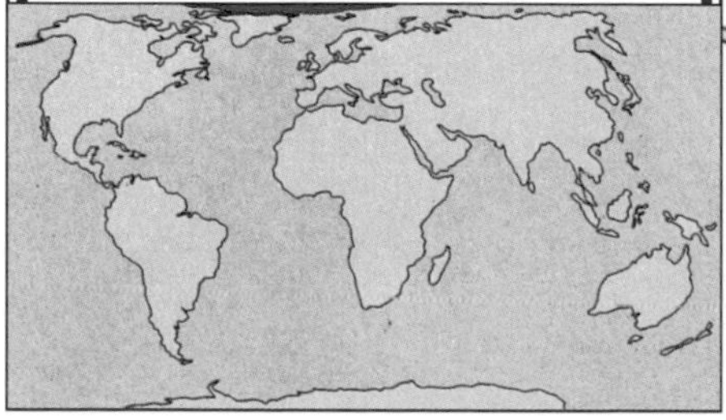

The Canadian Inuits, who live in the Arctic, invented the kayak, a skin-covered canoe.

Lapps, from the European Arctic, use reindeer to pull their sleds.

MILES	250	500	1000	1500	2000	2500	3000			
KILOMETRES	1000	1500	2000	2500	3000	3500	4000	4500	5000	

ANTARCTICA

Antarctica is at the bottom of the world. Unlike the frozen Arctic Ocean, Antarctica is actually ice-covered land. In some places the ice is 4,800 metres thick!

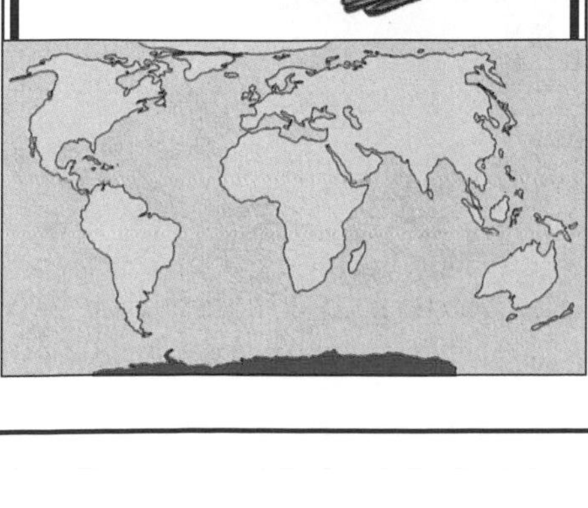

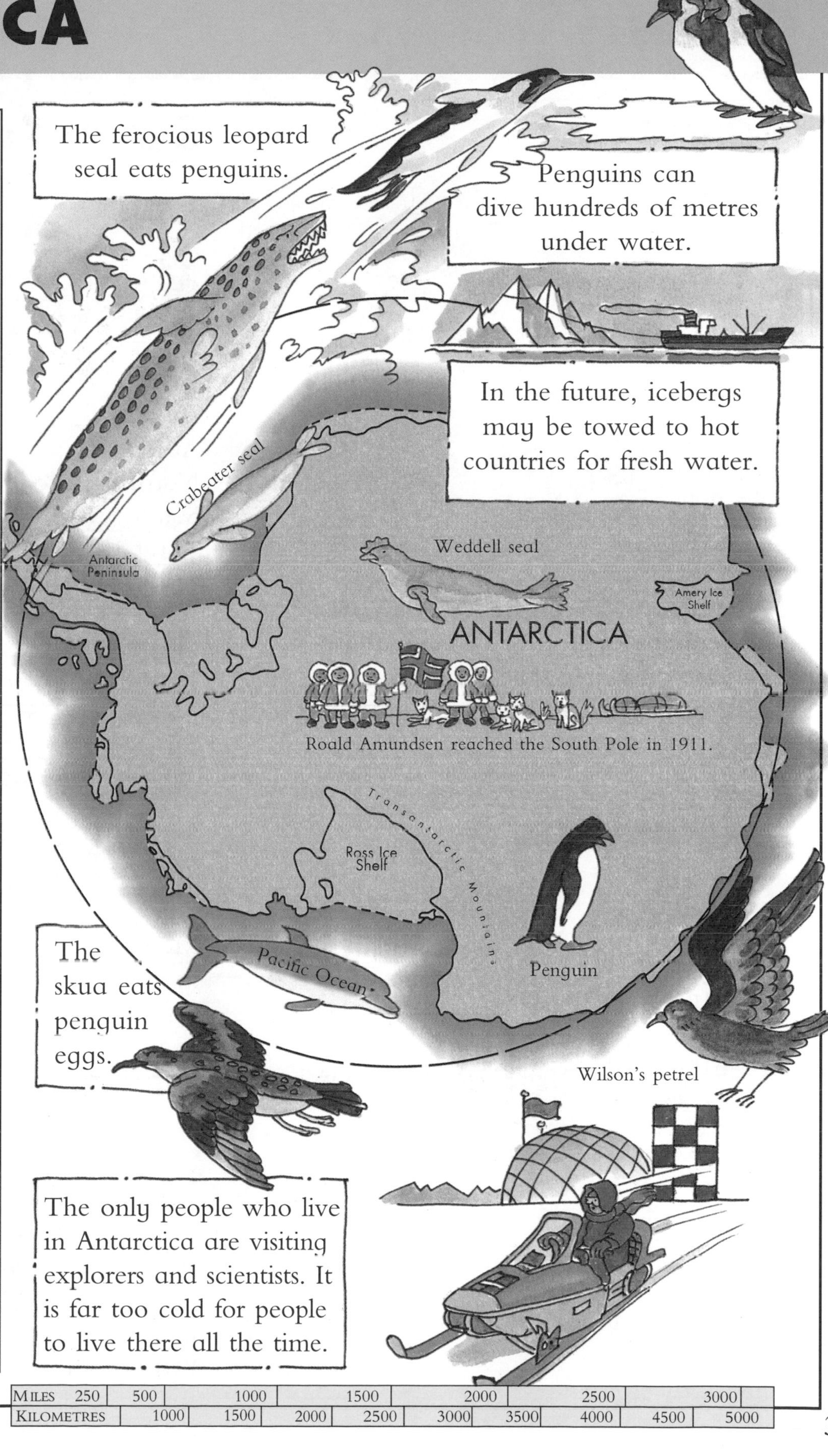

Crabeater seal
Antarctic Peninsula
Weddell seal
Amery Ice Shelf
ANTARCTICA
Roald Amundsen reached the South Pole in 1911.
Transantarctic Mountains
Ross Ice Shelf
Pacific Ocean
Penguin
Wilson's petrel

The ferocious leopard seal eats penguins.

Penguins can dive hundreds of metres under water.

In the future, icebergs may be towed to hot countries for fresh water.

The skua eats penguin eggs.

The only people who live in Antarctica are visiting explorers and scientists. It is far too cold for people to live there all the time.

MILES 250	500	1000		1500	2000		2500	3000	
KILOMETRES	1000	1500	2000	2500	3000	3500	4000	4500	5000

WORLD FACTS

COLDEST

Antarctica is the coldest place in the world. It can be as cold as -89°C.

OCEANS

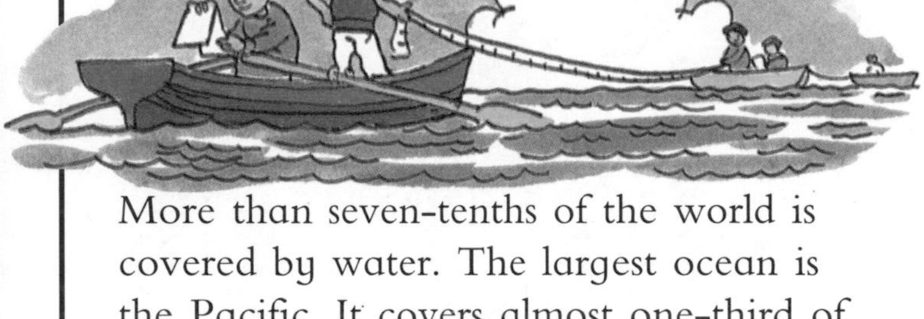

More than seven-tenths of the world is covered by water. The largest ocean is the Pacific. It covers almost one-third of the Earth's surface – 166,240,900 sq km.

EARTHQUAKES

Some parts of the world have more earthquakes than others. They are near faults, where pieces of land rub against each other, making the ground tremble. San Francisco, USA, is built near a fault and suffers from earthquakes.

SIZE OF CONTINENTS

Asia	43,565,000 sq km
Africa	30,262,000 sq km
North America	23,400,000 sq km
South America	17,806,000 sq km
Antarctica	14,000,000 sq km
Europe	10,521,000 sq km
Australia	7,686,000 sq km

WETTEST

Mawsynram, in India, is the wettest place in the world. Every year it has over 1,160 millimetres of rain.

DRIEST

In 1971, part of the Atacama Desert, in Peru, had its first rainfall in 400 years.

DESERTS

The Sahara in North Africa is the largest desert in the world. It covers an area bigger than Australia!

MOUNTAINS

The highest mountain in the world is Mount Everest on the China/Nepal border. It is 8,848 metres high.

LARGEST COUNTRIES

Russia	17,075,400 sq km
Canada	9,976,139 sq km
China	9,565,961 sq km
USA	9.372,614 sq km
Brazil	8,511,965 sq km

HOTTEST

One of the hottest places in the world is Death Valley in California, USA. Temperatures there can climb higher than 54°C.

VALLEYS

The Marianas Trench is a valley at the bottom of the Pacific Ocean. With a depth of 12,143 metres, it is the deepest valley in the world.

VOLCANOES

There are 200 active volcanoes in Indonesia.

INDEX